Freya Stark (1893–1993), 'the poet of travel', was the doyenne of Middle East travel writers and one of the most courageous and adventurous women travellers of her generation. She travelled extensively throughout Syria, Palestine, Lebanon, Iran, Iraq and Southern Arabia, where she became the first western woman to travel through the Hadhramaut. Usually alone, she ventured to places few Europeans had visited. Her travels earned her the title of Dame and huge public acclaim. Her many, now classic, books include *Traveller's Prelude*, *Ionia*, *The Southern Gates of Arabia*, *Alexander's Path*, *Dust in the Lion's Paw*, *East is West* and *Valleys of the Assassins*.

'It was rare to leave her company without feeling that the world was somehow larger and more promising. Her life was something of a work of art... The books in which she recorded her journeys were seductively individual... Nomad and social lioness, public servant and private essayist, emotional victim and mythmaker.'

Colin Thubron, *The New York Times*

'Few writers have the capacity to do with words what Faberge could do with gems – to fashion them, without violating their quality. It is this extraordinary talent which sets Freya Stark apart from her fellow craftsman in the construction of books on travel.'

The Daily Telegraph

'Freya Stark remains unexcelled as an interpreter of brief encounters in wild regions against the backdrop of history.'   *The Observer*

'It is... as the writer of beautiful, measured prose rather than as a traveller or as an exotic 'character' who wore Dior in the wilder reaches of Asia and Arabian dress in London, that Freya Stark will ultimately be remembered.'   *The Independent*

'One of the finest travel writers of our century.'   *The New Yorker*

'A Middle East traveler, an explorer and, above all, a writer, Freya Stark has, with an incomparably clear eye, looked toward the horizon of the past without ever losing sight of the present. Her books are route plans of a perceptive intelligence, traversing time and space with ease.'   *Saudi Aramco World*

Tauris Parke Paperbacks is an imprint of I.B.Tauris. It is dedicated to publishing books in accessible paperback editions for the serious general reader within a wide range of categories, including biography, history, travel and the ancient world. The list includes select, critically acclaimed works of top quality writing by distinguished authors that continue to challenge, to inform and to inspire. These are books that possess those subtle but intrinsic elements that mark them out as something exceptional.

The Colophon of Tauris Parke Paperbacks is a representation of the ancient Egyptian ibis, sacred to the god Thoth, who was himself often depicted in the form of this most elegant of birds. Thoth was credited in antiquity as the scribe of the ancient Egyptian gods and as the inventor of writing and was associated with many aspects of wisdom and learning.

THE MINARET
OF DJAM

An Excursion in Afghanistan

Freya Stark

TAURIS PARKE
PAPERBACKS

Reprinted in 2011 by Tauris Parke Paperbacks

New paperback edition published in 2010 by Tauris Parke Paperbacks
An imprint of I.B.Tauris and Co Ltd
6 Salem Road, London W2 4BU
175 Fifth Avenue, New York NY 10010
www.ibtauris.com

Distributed in the United States and Canada Exclusively by Palgrave Macmillan
175 Fifth Avenue, New York NY 10010

First published in 1970 by John Murray (Publishers) Limited

Cover image: 'Minaret of Djam, UNESCO World Heritage Site, dating from the
twelfth century, with Quasr Zarafshan in background, Ghor Province, Afghanistan'
© Jane Sweeney/Robert Harding

ISBN: 978 1 84885 313 3

A full CIP record for this book is available from the British Library
A full CIP record is available from the Library of Congress

Library of Congress Catalog Card Number: available

Printed and bound in the UK by CPI Antony Rowe, Chippenham and Eastbourne

Contents

Illustrations

Photographs

All photographs not otherwise acknowledged are by the author

Drawings

Author's Note

This book makes no claim to be anything but a travel diary: there is a wide choice for further information, but the works chiefly consulted here in a general way and not marked by footnotes are:

The new *Encyclopaedia of Islam*

W. K. Fraser-Tytler: *Afghanistan* (Oxford University Press, 1967)

C. E. Bosworth: *The Ghaznevids* (Edinburgh University Press, 1963)

P. Macrory: *Signal Catastrophe* (Hodder, 1966)

Arnold Toynbee: *Between Oxus and Jumna* (Oxford University Press, 1961)

W. W. Tarn: *The Greeks and Bactria* (Cambridge, 1957)

Sir Aurel Stein: *On Alexander's Track to the Indus* (Macmillan, 1929)

I would like here to add to the gratitude I owe to my companions, my thanks for the use of Mark's drawings and Claire's two minaret photographs.

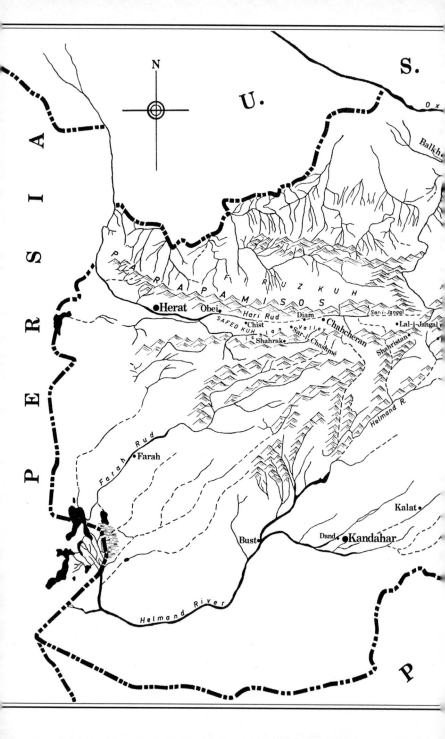

1

Four Roads

Eight years ago, they told me, there was not a modern building in Kabul. Adventurous modernity now pushes out among booths that have come down from the Greek ages, and an untidy sprawling city struggles for form among the hills.

Box-like houses, mud or mud-brick, climb steeply beneath the walled precipitous skyline; they keep their rectangular shapes, with here and there unexpectedly well-set doors and windows that tell of the winter cold: one is apt to forget Kabul's snow while dust blows over pyramids of melons in her streets.

Thoroughfares are building with an eye to the future, but the country people still chiefly crowd the bazaars. They push by, with turbans askew round skull-caps gold-embroidered in Kandahar even for the poorest – the bright spot in their costume where everything else is the colour of dust. Their cotton trousers, unchanged from Sassanian or Parthian models, flop loose under a shirt to the knees, and a shorter western jacket worn above it takes away any stray look of splendour; it is in keeping with the rather dingy aspect of the long uneven streets.

After the first Afghan war of 1842, the second British expedition was ordered to carry out some sort of retaliation for the disasters suffered (through our own incompetence chiefly), and the ancient Kabul bazaar, the most uncomplaining object in sight, was destroyed. I remember, as a small child, hitting the chair over which I had stumbled, and the principle seems the same.

> And that dread city of Kabool,
>   Set at the mountains' very feet,
> Whose marble tanks are ever cool
>   With water in the summer heat,
>
> Where through the narrow dark bazaar
>   A little maid Circassian
> Is led, a present from the Czar . . .

All this has gone, but here and there bits of brightness remain in covered secluded openings where a Sikh or Punjabi sits black-bearded above satins and tinsel from Lahore. The 'remnant bazaar' holds the cast-off clothes of America among tumble-down streets, and some old Afghan will show his one-tooth smile as he handles a muslin ball-dress from Fifth Avenue, scarcely tarnished.

Beggars, one blind and led by his friend, are walking there to a long sing-song of their story – their brown faces, legs, arms, and rags of gowns coloured like the three-storeyed old wooden balconies above them, where camels used to pass into courtyards through shadowed gates, and men lie asleep in the half-dark. Squalid and thwarted with ruin, there is little beauty left except in faces, still lively as if flowering in dust.

The crowd jostles by, and Kabul gathers all the Afghan races: Pathans, probably mixed Aryan, neat-featured, black-bearded, black-turbaned; flat-faced Hazaras, whose unre-membered histories go back to Mongol armies; long Tajik profiles, Indo-Iranian, possibly original inhabitants from upper Oxus and across the Hindu Kush; or the bright eyes and uncombed heads of the pagan hillmen of Nuristan. Women, impeded by children or shopping, flit about under the fragile silk grille that hides their faces. The *chadari* makes their heads charmingly small and flairs round their ankles in a sprightly bell of *plissé* giving them a look of gaiety when they move: but when they stand shrouded on the sidewalk, seeing and unrecognized, the simile of the caryatid cannot but strike the passer-by; if she is a woman and addresses a kindly word to her shadowy sister across the barrier, it will give a never-failing shock to hear some French or English banality come from the unseen lips. The woman's life on the whole is the least happy aspect of Afghanistan, and it is the younger girls who are gay, walking about unimpeded; for them as for us the long skirt is out and mystery the last thing wanted[*]; yet it exists;

[*] This was written 1969.

and clothed in light or darkness the veiled caryatid, which the East through so many ages has secluded, can still remind a Westerner as he passes that the Unknown is at his side.

*   *   *

Unless one is out to draw maps or stalk the *Ovis Poli*, Afghanistan is a manageable country with only four asphalt roads to tempt the lazier tourist and not too many sites to crowd a traveller in his summer stay.

There is Balkh in the north – Bactria – once the greatest city of Central Asia, where Alexander left his invalids when he marched home; it flourishes gently, scarce a town now – a blossoming silence. Its area, enclosed by ramparts, is invaded by crops: pigeons year by year are destroying its one fine mosque, nesting in small fallen places of the mosaic tiles: its country wares on market-days are spread on carpets on the ground.

From its southern to its northern gate, between one-storeyed shops and houses, a straight road dozes under trees. Flocks nibble at the mounds of the great toothless walls. The windblown spaces of gateways once guarded look towards Oxus across the driving sand. In an empty grass-grown hotel, chairs are still dusted, and some travelling governor will be visited by landholders and *Arbabs* who come riding on their horses or in cars. I think of the Balkh hotel with tenderness because of the warmth of its welcome, in which human feeling was everything and mechanics – water or light, in buckets or lanterns – were kept to their subordinate places. We asked for two sheets instead of one to each bed and were delightedly provided – for we were guests, free of anything our generous hosts could give. The code of the guest, with duties on both sides, still holds in these quiet places, until 'modern comfort' in its most savage oriental shape destroys it.

The gate of India

The Mosque of Balkh

The Mosque of Balkh

The Mosque of Balkh: detail

The asphalt, which the Russians built from their frontier of the Oxus to Kabul, runs east through Kunduz, and a cross-country day is spent in reaching it from Balkh. Mazar-i-sharif and the shrine of Ali are on the way, with neon lights and orange flowerpots and domes like shallow turnips – where the seller of corn, seeing a stranger entranced among his doves, will throw a handful of his capital for nothing. I here subjugated a soldier who tried to turn me away as I stood barefoot at the shrine, by reciting the opening prayer for him from end to end.

The asphalt with its bulldozers was scouring this plain and has by now probably disturbed the dust and raftered bazaar of Tashkurgan. A year ago this was still a small township of the time when the Silk Road flourished, with the shape of the Mongol tents remembered in mud houses whose domes cluster round a dilapidated castle and its stream. From here the day is spent on the northern steppe, yellow or green according to the season; the cities of Bactriana lie sleeping underground. Professor Bernard and his French are excavating one of them (discovered by H. M. the present King, who is interested in archaeology): they work with the eye of the Russians upon them across Oxus, where the great river breaks from its 'bright mountain cradle of Pamir' into the Bactrian plain.

Long before reaching this we have returned to the Russian asphalt across the Kunduz ferry and its rich plain, and are sitting above the shaded main street of that prosperous little town, whose merchants stroll in striped silk coats with sleeves so stretched by fashion that they are thrown over the shoulders to flap about their ankles when they walk. On the tea-house veranda the belles of Pakistan are pasted in oleograph along the inside walls, and one can watch *tongas* of this horse-loving country streaking by brightly varnished, their ponies trotting smoothly, gay with red tassels from head to shoulder.

The Kunduz river now winds beside the road through puddings of earthy mountain on its way; it eats them like a worm, labouring from happy reaches that have pierced stonier and harder gorges into the Doshi plain.

Here, at Pul-i-Kumri, Bridge of Doves, is another and perhaps the pleasantest hotel in Afghanistan, with pine trees in a garden of tuberoses and geraniums. When the sun moves round, the garden wakes for the enchanted night; small electric bulbs begin to shine for the mere gaiety of shining among branches; the tuberose scent spreads rich and voluptuous; the gardener, leaving his hose to spill itself alone at the root of his roses, squats in a corner with the youngest of his many children and smokes the cigarette of the evening; the eldest makes the lawn neat by pulling grass into a sack to feed his goats. A waiter places plastic chairs and tin tables and smoothes the tablecloths upon them. The waiters are nearly all a family, from the Ghorband pass, except for one aquiline tousled young man from Nuristan; and they talk – about their marriages past or future – while a sparse clientèle gathers to sip its coffee here and there. A young lad will leap up, smile as he goes by, hitch his trousers with an ease of habit, and bend and kneel and stand to pray the evening prayer; and the moon sails overhead, from the tops of the pines to the roof of the hotel, as if it were part of the illumination of the garden. It looks domestic and small among the Afghan mountains: and indeed, before the scientific age that is turning it to its original dust and ashes, what brilliant intuition first guessed it to be bigger than any other lamp?

I spent three days in this sequestered place, drenched in stillness except for the soothing roar of a German-built dam near by. Few travellers came through, not more than one party a day, and we would talk to each other in the mornings, seated indoors among uncompromising armchairs while a fan went whirring through the heat – adventurous people driving to India or Nepal; women teachers out to see the sun-temple of Surkh Kotal that once overlooked these Hellenistic land-scapes;* sometimes an Afghan family moving to its summer hills from the heat of Kabul. When these short social intervals were over, the hours relapsed into their timeless serenity, and I came to think of them as part of History – the part that is never written – unnumbered days of unremembered people, my own among them.

The gorges above Doshi can be by-passed by the Ak-Robat pass, which is 12,500 feet high and usually clear of snow, and this and the Nil pass were the ancient ways north from Bamian, through a defile still called the Gate of India to Tashkurgan and Balkh. The excellent King Nadir Shah shortened the road in 1933 by cutting through the gorges, bisecting the Hindu Kush a little west of its watershed on the surprisingly low Shibar pass. Four or five passes east of this point were all more or less equally difficult, though the one taken by Alexander – the Khawak – at 11,640 feet, is also below the level of perpetual snow; but there was little to choose between them all until the Russians carried through their second attempt† upon them from the Salang heights. No longer is it almost indifferent which route a traveller might choose in country so difficult and dangerous; the Salang runs to a tunnel up its long tilted funnel of a valley, with peaks as high but not as lovely as the highest Alps on either hand; then winds down between mountain villages like wasps' nest clusters, to the plain of Kabul, the cynosure of armies, and the dip to the Indus. As one loops down, the old road on the right to Bamian and the north, and west to Herat, takes off. But the Russian road

---

* Built under Kanishka who succeeded the Bactrian Greeks
† The first in 1929. See Fraser-Tytler for the geography.

carries on to Kabul through the plain where the Afghan takes over for Khyber and Peshawar and the Indian El Dorado beyond.

These are the two main roads of east Afghanistan, and one could be drawn to loiter towards the Khyber and perhaps follow the disastrous southern detour that led the British troops to die with one solitary survivor at the last gap near Jalalabad in 1842. After hunting in vain in the prosperous little tropic town for tracings of the lines successfully held there, one follows the modern asphalt among small square forts that still bristle on every hill; until the names of regiments are reached, British, Pathan, or Indian, carved on jutting rocks where years and blood lie eaten by the sun. The spick and span Pakistanis hold the frontier, closing it before evening as we taught them; and the painted lorries wait at the top of the pass.

> *Tutto è pace e silenzio e tutto posa*
> *Il mondo e più di lor non si ragiona.* [*]

John Lawrence was in favour of an Afghanistan reaching to the Indus, and I think I would have been and still am of his mind; yet the devotion which held that border and fought and was trusted by enemy and friend is a quality never to be disdained by nations fortunate enough to have had it written in their annals.

My travelling heart, however, was set not to the east, but from Kabul westward, where Afghanistan's other two main roads lead to Kandahar and then to Herat. What chiefly interested me were not the main roads at all, but the east-west traverse of the mountains between them, from Kabul to Herat by the minaret of Djam. This beautiful and secluded piece of

[*] All is now peace and silence and the world settles to rest nor speaks of them again. G. Leopardi: *La Sera del dì di festa.*

thirteenth-century architecture was accidentally discovered some eleven years ago and could be reached by a Land-Rover; and I had returned to Afghanistan in the summer of 1968 to reach it if I could.

When I got to Kabul I discovered that my journey would mean either a horse which would take too long, or the hiring of a Land-Rover and driver which I could not afford. I therefore resigned myself to the inevitable, settled happily in Kabul – kindly helped by the British Council in general and Ken and Lydie Pearson in particular – and in their garden, with Mr Ramazan, an excellent Afghan-Persian teacher, worked through the cooler hours, while their gardener, robed in green like some unimportant rural god, poured unceasing water on the rather passive flowers – for we had reached the middle of July. The Pearson servants would move about the house with mountain strides too ample for a city staircase, and bring cherry juice in tumblers to mitigate the heat.

People came out of their doors when the climax of the afternoon was over, and I would come from my siesta and find them in the garden rehearsing *Twelfth Night* for an Embassy performance in a few weeks' time. Ken was producing it; and day after day the rather uncoordinated elements of English-speaking Kabul could be seen and heard welding themselves into the not so very dissimilar social background of Illyria. It is remarkable how naturally Shakespeare fits the East; as far as Venice, as he travels out from Europe, he presents the splendid Renaissance in his productions, but in India, or Kabul, or Istanbul or Baghdad there is no necessity to labour an atmosphere: it is already in the air we breathe, in the cruelty, poverty, gaiety and philosophy of the bazaar, in the Unexpected ready to happen round every corner – not padded out with insurances as we try to circumvent it, but nakedly electric, a sword out of the sheath.

I would watch the English boys and girls gradually peeling off the centuries and finding – some more some less – their own tradition clothed in words that had once been familiar, to be as it were re-discovered, to fit easily, to become once again a natural self-expression with every repetition as the days went by. Sometimes the wind blew and the green and silver poplar leaves tossed and glittered like sequins through dust round the garden walls; sometimes the pale sunset was left undisturbed to soak everything in its yellow light; and this was Illyria, and anything might happen, and Viola – a slim little boyish slip in her working jeans – was saying things about love that everyone should know. The thought of what we are and to what we are turning, and how long our today has been in the making, would move about in my head as I watched and listened. It continued to do so, more and more, in the days to come.

Claire and Mark turned up one afternoon to look at the rehearsal. Old to the young and young to me, they had the spring-cleaned look that a return to hot baths and easy bedrooms gives to the dusty traveller of the East. He had driven a Land-Rover from Europe and was planning to spend some time in Afghanistan, and we were talking in no time of the cross-country journey by the minaret of Djam, my unaccomplished dream. How enviable! We counted routes and days and how many would be required, and looked at maps unobtainable in Kabul; and presently Claire said, 'Why don't you come with us? We have an empty seat.'

It took her, she told me later, about five minutes to make up her mind to invite me; and I had perhaps a minute's hesitation and mentioned Francis, who was arriving next day. Seats for us both were available, said Claire; the party would consist of us four and Zalmia the cook, who could drive a car (not that he was ever allowed to do so), and speak a little English.

There was a problem about dates, because Francis had the ending of a three weeks' leave and our ambassador, who was being helpful and charming, was anxious that there should be two Land-Rovers more or less together to help each other over the uncertain patches of the track. A Psychologist was coming from England to fish in the river of Djam, and would we wait till all could go together? We agreed to do so; Francis and I put in the time in Bamian and the north, and we came back to find the scientist and his party just arriving.

*   *   *

The travellers all met at lunch in the Embassy, which stands in splendid and solid isolation, far from all the other embassies, in a garden of lawns and giant planes and roses: it was built when the last Afghan war was over, and the expensive English wisecrack that Britain loses every battle except the last was presumably invented; but the giant plane trees continue to grow, ever more beautiful and more perfectly rounded in their native soil, while the empire that planted them has become a thin voice of the air. There is still nevertheless an atmosphere of stability, a country-house sort of spaciousness and ease, and an excellent library of its period, to make the Afghanistan embassy one of the most desirable posts in the world for anyone who likes to get away from the insecurities of Europe.

Coming from the Poet's daily perennial words, it seemed to me that our tradition here also was still visible and recently active, though obviously dormant now: and as our party sat at luncheon, I wondered idly to which channel of our stream we too belonged – transitory or perpetual? The Ambassador was all right, I thought; he was chatting pleasantly with bright, observant, unselfconscious eyes that dealt with the world as it came, and he had recovered from his annoyance with the

Psychologist's secretary, who had kept all the guests waiting
and come down in a mini-skirt far too short, and had been sent
back to change. The Ambassadress, at the other end of the
table, was safe too: she is American, with beautiful untidy hair
and long hands that wave spontaneously about, like fronds of
water-flowers in the gentle casualness of her thoughts; what
world can it ever be that finds no place for a woman genuinely
pleasant, good-looking and kind? On either side of her were
Ken and the Turkish professor, the most distinguished of the
other party apart from Bill Allen, an old friend from Cairo
who sat by me and kept me happy talking of Mithridates;
tradition took us upstream as it were, two thousand years or
so where it was young. The Turkish professor had swum the
Oxus to escape out of Central Asia from Russia in his youth,
and had come to revisit Balkh after forty years. His appearance
chiefly expressed a benign absorption. Ken, on the far side,
with fine-drawn, harassed profile, was obviously of the Poet's
company whatever their separation in Time. Lydie, his wife,
dipping into the household world where someone has to see
about the dinners, made an art of the average life, and so
did Mark, beside her: he had the charming oddity of a mouth
turned down at the corners which yet looked ready to smile –
a long rectangular face, blue eyes, modest but resolute on
occasion, fearless to where the imagination carried, and that
might be quite far; in the next two weeks of our journey I
never had to alter this opinion. Claire sat opposite, everything
about her neat, cosy, and determined; her head – sleek and
grey with a black band to hold it – agreed with a general
appearance of relaxed efficiency, as of a small round planet
moving methodically through its own spaces. Her brown eyes
were round like those of a trustful little furry animal – soft
when pleased and easily pleased. She had spent her life among

Top: Balkh. North gate looking to the Oxus
Bottom: Way to the Salang pass

On the Charikar road

The fort of Kabul

Emperor Babur's tomb in Kabul

archives in various countries, and had now retired, and was out to see the world.

Francis, young himself, sat next the young secretary, who looked rather as if deep were appealing to deep in a company where everyone else must have seemed old. My sympathy for anyone sent from the dining-room to change was I think wasted; whatever traditions of a worn-out code were ruling the rest of us, she belonged to the generation that had scrapped them; she smouldered beside Francis, discussing racialism in Australia, perhaps finding his rather abstract linguistic interests unrewarding, while I thought about her in a uselessly maternal way. How hard it must be to have to appear tougher than you are, and to go round the stray corners of the world with people whose hearts are shallow as far as you are concerned; and to have nothing you wish to be or do that you will risk your life for the reaching of; and to have a face that is pretty only for a time.

As for the Psychologist, he was tall and slim, and got what he wanted by never wanting the unattainable – not one to look about and linger, or picture vagueness beyond the invisible horizons. His Afghan Land-Rover, whose business it was to take millionaires to look for *Ovis Poli* in Nuristan, had been going through all the prima-donna tricks that an oriental car indulges in before an expedition starts, and a certain cheerful but indubitable impatience could be detected in his brisk house-guest politeness among values so much less neatly defined than his own.

There we all were, drops in a stream that had conveyed us through the ages, shaping us from one origin into our multiform variety. Yet apart from the Psychologist, who looked upon localities as made for his use while he was in them and Afghanistan as much of a background as anywhere else, we all shared one element of our tradition – an easy adaptation to foreign places, whose eccentricities we enjoyed while not surrendering our own. This perhaps had been a secret of empire while it lasted; and the controversial subject of tradition, its misreading and its constitution, its pitfalls, powers and validities, stayed with me as we set out next morning for the crossing to Herat.

2

Enhancements of Life

T he other party, having delays over their car, were following to overtake us at Panjau (Five Waters); and as our
chief wish was to travel slowly, we decided to make a two-day
journey of it, camping by the Helmand river on the way.

We started at 7.30 on the eighth of August, and Kabul was already well on with its morning business as we threaded the last slovenly houses and came out in sight of the mountains that haunt this city, not too near but not far, on every side. Deep in snow in winter, a dusty cloud is apt to hide them in summer, when even the stars are dusty in Kabul; but when the mist shreds apart, the fairness of rock shines through, as if it were the shoulder of a goddess and not the thick vaulting of our world. Visible or invisible, the mountains can never be forgotten, since they are the reason of the city's existence. In east and south-east they drop headlong down the gorges where sixteen thousand men with their women and their new-born babies set out on the 6th day of January 1842 for their certain destruction. In the north and north-east the Hindu Kush raises its faint far head as it soars to the Great Pamir and on to Himalaya. From every quarter – Balkh, Peshawar, Jalalabad, Quetta or Kandahar – Kabul is in the way, a city to be defended or conquered. Kapisa, Alexander's city, and Begram, the Kushan capital that followed it, were built near by in the same essential opening of the hills; and Babur, first of the Mogul emperors, came back from the subjected Indian plains to lie under its wall beneath his marble sword. This charming and endearing person, carrying numerous aunts and other female relatives about with him through his conquests and disasters, wrote one of the best autobiographies ever written in any language, and bandied verses with his generals.

We left all this, in the direction of Kandahar, and soon abandoned the American asphalt and the wide natural trough made for the marching of armies, and turned to easy dusty country where black oxen were treading the harvest. We kept steadily west along the way to Bamian, towards the Unai pass through gently sloping, cultivated plains rare in Afghanistan, that give a sense of relaxation in the strenuous land. The more northerly route to Bamian, turning off from the Kabul (Kuh-i-Daman) plain above Charikar, follows the long narrow valley of the Ghorband river to Shibar pass from which it springs; having only a 9,240 foot height to cross, it is often open in winter, and its road winds from riverside villages with fruit-tree gardens – plum, apricot, apple, peach and almond – into a tangle of sheltered gorges, the Shumbol, the Bololah, the Shikari. The rich and peaceful Bamian valley, opening from them, was protected by two fortresses at the narrows of the east, impregnable until the armies of Chingiz Khan destroyed them. A silence then fell upon the valley where he passed. The three-tiered walls of Zohak the Red City melted into huge bastions of the mud that built them, and Sar-i-Koshak, the Shikari castle, is now scarce visited while the lorries that make for Doshi thread their way beneath it to avoid the heights of the Salang road. Golgola, the metropolis of the valley, spreads destroyed like an anthill on its mound, and looks across flat land to the equally ruined, multitudinous black termite holes that were monks' cells in the face of the northern cliffs.

The huge and, let us face it, ugly Buddhas, shorn of their paint and gold, look out with absent minds, if any, and that rather lymphatic plumpness of Gandhara: their shadows mark the passage of the sun in the wide and fertile valley which is now inhabited but no longer dedicated – though a climate of meditation lingers. The winters cover it with an added silence of deep snow. I spent many hours here, looking from a promontory where a small hotel is built over a view like that in some medieval breviary, with the year and all its seasons illustrated. The hotel enjoyed a straight avenue of willows soft-edged and round as clouds, but the peasants' road came down in sight, from angle to angle and village to village, from

walls and gates and corner towers half lost in trees: by some
strange contrast, those blind defensive walls, with gates left
open and hay carts in and out, dripped peace like honey –
Mandragora and all the drowsy syrups of this world. The uneven
ways were sunk between dry walls to keep animals from
straying into crops – potatoes, or oats' harvested stubble, or
sweet-scented pink clover; and here in the early morning the
peasants, men and women, would walk in slow files up their
hills. They carried all they needed for the day's work – their
sickle and a kettle or an amphora for water, some bread no
doubt, and a quilted cotton to wrap the meagre harvest which,
in the evening light, they carried home. A boundless, timeless
dignity embraced this small procession, whose dingy shirts
and turbans – mere dust in Kabul streets – here managed to
absorb the majesty of earth. Step behind step, as they reached
the slope, their shoulders bent under the load, they dinted the
steep land with their rough sandals, leaving marks scarcely
more ephemeral than their own selves, while the ravished
valley lapped them round, quiet, lovely and austere as the
first sleep of death, with features neither absent nor present,
composed and divorced for ever.

In the evening, as the colour faded and the wind from
Hindu Kush blew regularly till eight or so, the northern
ridges which the daylight of the sun had hidden seemed to
sweep down towards the vertical Buddha cliffs and the valley's peace. Their precipices were flattened by perspective
and the lenient light into declivities gently descending, made
visibly unreachable only through the fierceness of their outline in the sky. The Buddha cliffs were scored by gothic clefts
and shadows that had turned into sculpture long before first
a chisel was invented – processions of earlier gods immobile
but alive. 'Era l'ora che volge il desio', the backward-looking
hour; the traffic of the great valley road and the innumerable

feet of pilgrims hung faint as the echo of a flute where these ancient sorrows were forgotten. I thought of a book beloved in my childhood called *Sintram and his Companions* and the Dürer drawing that inspired it, where, with Satan innocuous and the tumults of hatred behind them, the Knight and Death rode through the reconciled landscape and the labours of the year.

From Bamian there is a track over high pastures to five deep sapphire lakes set in hills that can look white in the noonday light. What the Americans call a dirt-track goes on to the Five Waters; but it is the longer way and more dusty, and we all knew it, so that we left the Unai-Bamian road as it crosses the Helmand and makes by a second pass for the Kalu river and the ruins of the Red City on its crag. This pass crosses the eastern end of the Kuh-i-Baba range which rises to 5,143 metres and was to become for the next two days our skyline to the north. We saw it from Unai as we crossed the watershed between the Kabul river and the Helmand.

The chief memory of the approach to Unai was the gradual disappearance of trees. It is a long narrow valley with uneventful sides open to the sun, and the lush cultivation gradually vanishes into its arid shape, as if it were the open half of a funnel covered by the sky. The houses get scarce and vanish also, and cease to bury their holy men with flags of rags stuck on bamboos to note them. Where the waterways still run under poplars we stopped at the last good-sized village beside a plot of flowers, and drank tea out of bowls, with a Japanese teapot beside each customer, under a wayside awning; and the sun had climbed to its meridian before we saw one of the painted lorries that travel as buses across the Afghan hills, askew among camels in front of the highest caravanserai. From here the pass goes on in rising humps of rounded earth or shale, speckled with prickly cushions of *acantholimon* (or *acanthophyllum*).

One could fill many volumes with the enhancements of life, not the things themselves but the accidents that surround and give them as it were their iridescence. Sometimes these light upon, and show, the essential secret, like moonlight on the heights of Taygetus, awakening the silver mica of its summits in the night; but there are also fortuitous enhancements which clothe their characters with oddities or dignities foreign to their essential selves and to enjoy which a touch of inconsistency and surprise is required. These belong in a particular way to the casual roadside and are different in kind from those other adventures in reality that discover what truly exists, or awaken things long known but not remembered. When I returned to England towards the end of the Second World War, I revisited my Dartmoor home and called at one of our little farms whose master I had known as a boy. 'He will be out with the sheep,' they said, and I walked through the familiar land and across the turf to find him; when I reached him among his flock, although twenty years had passed, he said, 'I thought it was you, Miss Freya, coming along over the hill.'

Such meetings delve deep into our sources or into those of others, and their appeal is not due to what I like to call the enhancements of chance. But the flicker of a conversation on the road from stranger to stranger, that picks its magic as if out of the air, can endure though nothing particular was said: the unknown background, the gaiety of the day, the mere delight of living, have splashed it with illusion.

This happened at the top of the pass. The view opened and showed the Helmand valley and the range of Kuh-i-Baba on its farther side, and on our right the tip of a rounded hill with a mud watch-tower alone and disused against the sky. Height sparkled in everything – sky, cloud, and brightness of stone, the taste of the air, the whispering lapse of almost invisible water, and cheerful optimism of yellow flowers like stemless

Zohak. The Red City below Bamian

The Bamian river in Bololah gorge

Bamian. The lesser Buddha

The eastern Buddha cliff in the Bamian valley

Bamian. Bazaar

Below the Unai pass

Afghan lorry

Helmand valley below Unai

dandelions: afraid of the winds they clung with limpet-like Victorian propriety and very strong roots to their mother earth. There was lavender about, and chickory and convolvulus and that blue and white herbaceous plant whose stem is delicately square – motionless now in the strong cool light of noon, but slender enough to bend in any breeze, like the jewelled flowers the ladies of Istanbul once wore among their laces.

In the dip where the water started, a lorry was resting, its crew washing their faces delicately so as not to muddy the shallowness of the tributary; and though we only exchanged a few greetings and a word or two about the valley road before us, the scene remains in my memory bright with the lorry's painted mottoes and doves and fancies, an enhancement incongruous but gay among the worn, sun-drenched unpopulated summits, as if a butterfly were to have settled on the ridged features of Voltaire.

We lunched here and slipped steeply down to the Helmand and, at about 2.30, at a bridge and few houses and a caravanserai where the Bamian road leaves it, followed westward down the valley with the stream beside us. Its pebbles showed brown through the water, and the current marked it down the middle with little scimitars of light. Groves of soft willows and clumps of poplar were scattered with scarce villages and little cultivation, a few horses grazing and the valley on the north rising in wide pastoral folds to hide Kuh-i-Baba's battlemented edges. The afternoon lay curled like a cat asleep, and we travelled downstream westward, with the world too moving towards its rest.

The discovery that Mark was the leader of our party had soon been made: he would listen in an abstract way to two or three of our alternatives before taking the pipe out of his mouth and making whatever suggestion seemed finally right.

When we stopped, he immediately unloaded cushions or beds to rest on, rugs, sunshades, or whatever was required, and thought of himself not merely last but not at all. At about 3.30 he stopped where the road turns inland, drove the Land-Rover across flat grass to the water's edge, and suggested that we might enjoy what was left of the afternoon and camp here for the night.

A first enchanted evening therefore found our beds set out on grass nibbled short by herds all summer. The river ran close by with unobtrusive noises, sudden gurgles of hurry, nosing along its earthy walls like the musk-rat in the *Jungle Book* that never reached the middle of the room. How lucky is a stream, I thought as I lay idly, that has no need to repeat its rounds over the same ground like most of us, looking for something it never finds, but knows its way and eats through the hills that impede it. And yet those poor Afghan rivers are frustrated enough, for the thirsty lands drink them as they flow westward and lose them at last in the sands of Khurasan: and my mind ran through the hills that lay before us, and across the flattening steppes that melt into the pathless horizon, and the Lut with its whirlpools of salt and sand. Zalmia the cook, near by, squatting over our supper, inspired the primus to its little sizzle of contentment in the sunset air, and the homing black cows lifted their heads and moved their submissive flanks slowly, and snuffed at the ford as they waded through it with a boy behind them. A hamlet of four houses was the centre of this small world, tucked at the foot of a promontory of rock and shale: Dané-Ausela they called it, but the map suggests Kizil-Bashi (Red-head) and the traveller can choose – as indeed he can with most of the smaller eastern names: they seldom agree with their maps, which never agree with each other.

Nothing happened in the hamlet through the daylight hours. What was described as a hotel offered a covered balcony for our beds, for which the warm air showed no need; and now and then a woman would linger round a door-post where the female authority stopped.

As the evening closed in, a company came by us, walking with their eyes on the water beside a fisherman and his net. He threw it when he saw a dark enough shadow, with the movement that has come down through Greek vases and, every time, the little weights that fringed it made a perfect circle on his pool. The young lads told us their supper was found when they stopped to greet us, but threw once more for our sake, and seven little silver fish, as if it were an Arabian Nights' story, were caught in the net for the guests. The place then sank into darkness with one light shining until, about ten at night, a jeep came down from nowhere, and the balcony that had been offered us was presently filled with sleeping figures rolled in their quilts with their heads covered like cocoons. Out of range of all this I lay snug in the Land-Rover, which Mark had turned into a curtained room; through the open door I looked over the beds of my companions below me, under a moon whose light the valley seemed to lap up as blotting paper does ink, making it obscure. The sweet out-of-door drowsiness wrapped me as if it were a part of the mountain darkness, and the river lisped and murmured between its invisible banks. It knows its own direction, I thought, and remembered a poem written long ago – 'Deep in my heart direction lies' – if we can follow that, we move safely and any road can lead us, carrying through the darkness, like the Helmand, our own secret climate of repose.

3

Sheep

My two friends and the Land-Rover, whose cherishing made it almost human, were the happiest trio for travel, their human possessivenesses subdued by habit and harmony to an easy vagueness: the days hammered their routine, and Francis and I slipped into it without causing more disturbance than the gentleness of their care for me must have entailed.

Francis was young and assumed to look after himself, which he did in a dedicated way, eating, drinking, shaving, packing with amiable intensity while Claire and Mark did the work. When Zalmia had come forward with mugs of tea from a bubbling kettle, our two hosts in their turn would stroll with soap and towels to find some inlet at the river's bend. Francis by then was ready, though still with mug in hand – but all was finished. I had done nothing at all. It was a holiday, they told me. The only virtue left was punctuality, and I slipped out early. Dust or vapour smouldered like slabs of iron still hot on the black horizon, and grasses invisible brushed against my feet. But quickly, while I dressed, peak beyond peak, slope beyond slope caught the light, descending as a lover's hand tender and victorious down the delicate backbone ridges. Oh breathing world! I stepped into it to the sound of the kettle's humming, to find Claire ready to offer her bed to be reclined on.

Claire and Mark's timetable provided tea on waking, with a proper breakfast an hour or two later on the way: a major meal came some time in the afternoon when camp was set, combining lunch and supper. This was an improvement on my own system, which has given me forty frustrated years over the matter of breakfast, trying to persuade muleteers or guides in various nations to have it ready in time: we left at 6 a.m. with the day still harmless and innocently warm before us.

The Helmand, like most rivers and human histories, has reaches that never remain long uninterrupted, and just below our pastoral camp it begins to tumble to its gorges: but we climbed inland in shallow spirals that had given little trouble to those who first trod them – flocks of Chingiz Khan and of many before him, for we were stepping up into an ageless land. The lower margins of the hills, where the lift of the valleys reached them, began to be outlined by innumerable

thin lines that kept as much as possible along a level – tracks
of sheep or goats if close together or wider-spaced for kine.

When, in our 11th and 13th centuries, the Turkish ancestors came down from the steppes of Mongolia, there was no
personal malice, but merely a necessity for the grazing of innumerable flocks. The civilizations of Central Asia went down
before them and have not yet recovered, and never again have
sheep been as momentous as here in the human story. Towns
with their fruit trees and gardens were not needed and irri-
gated pasture was scarce; and there is a description of how
the strong, squat, slant-eyed soldiers dealt with city walls:
the loop of a long rope would be passed inside, coming out
through two holes with a distance between them, and the two
halves of the army would pull at the two ends of the rope till
mud towers and the houses behind them fell in ruin and the
rope came through.

So the cities vanished – often never to be reborn – Tirmidh,
Balkh, and Merv and Urgench; and the plain of Central Asia in
spite of all later prosperities and resurrections still holds the
atmosphere of ruin, though many walls have been rebuilt and
gardens planted. There is a passage by a Chinese traveller who
passed by Balkh when he visited Chingiz Khan and crossed
the Oxus in A.D. 1222.[*] The inhabitants had been taken and
massacred in cold blood some days before, and the travellers
camped outside, 'but we could still hear dogs barking in its
streets.' Today the flocks, the blunt-nosed goats ahead and
white or black sheep behind them, keep to the outskirts of the
cultivated plains.

We were ascending into such a shared territory, and a dozen
times or more in the following days would meet these rippling
crowds. The black lambs whose karakul coats are one of the

---

[*] *The Travels of an Alchemist*, translated by Arthur Waley; Routledge 1931 and
1963.

chief Afghan exports would sport over the slopes or wrinkled boulders, unconscious of their happiness in not being ripped from their mothers' wombs like the more expensive fur. Their shearing, done very roughly, left them tousled with a touch of modern bravado, very different from the dowdiness of the older generation plodding placidly with waddling tails in the middle of the dust. I have stood where the front leader of such a line happened to hit my shadow. He stopped, with his nose to the ground, and so did all his followers behind him. The sun was blazing on either side of my blackness and the road was open but – never raising their heads to see what was halting them – the sheep remained immobile and so did I. Intrigued by the situation, I let about five minutes pass and then removed my shadow; and the sheep flowed on, no doubt satisfied with a docility that had once gained them the whole of Central Asia.

The go-ahead Russians now transport their sheep from pasture to pasture by air, but the Afghans still walk them to their grazing grounds – perhaps a ten days' march or so, three times in the course of the year. Their shepherds are wrapped against the sun in all the rags they can lay hold of, and seasoned to a mahogany darkness through which their teeth shine when they smile. But they do so rarely, busy as they are pitting their authority against the panic inspired by even a stationary car. Mark, sucking his pipe in a purposeful way, would ease us through the tumult as it seethed by in soft smells of wool and dust – feet pattering out of sight with a noise like water jostling among those frightened boulders, whose yielding sides could have no notion of the regal immobilities of stone.

These nomad detachments met us at intervals, always on their way into some side valley, for we had come to patches of cultivated downland, spread out on both sides of the Helmand cleft. The upper levels tumbled like dolphins round the ark of Kuh-i-Baba in the north, whose three highest summits, elevated on a pedestal of rock, reminded me of those trinities of temples in the dead Roman towns of Tunisia, lifted above the open spaces of their Curiae and the forgotten municipal buildings of their day. Three prongs of snow clung as if the sky were striking the rising earth with a trident; and we travelled all morning looking across the summer-bleached ranges to this prodigious view.

After about two hours' driving we found a grassy dip where the beginnings of water are carried by a small *jub*, *juy* or ditch immediately along the gentlest gradient to feed some lower cluster of tents or houses or merely fields. Poplars or willows outline the banks of these small life-givers, but we were high up near the very source of water, and except for a village clump or two saw scarcely a tree all day. Hoopoes in great numbers inhabited our corner, moving over its rocks with the strut of Spanish dancers, a feathery crown giving the poise of a lace mantilla or high comb. Wagtails, rollers, green-gold bee-eaters, the white and black kingfisher, were all seen on this day; and wherever the barley had ripened, flocks of small birds would open their wings with a flash of yellow waistcoat, and twitter along to other harvests near by. An essence of delight, austere but easy, lay all about us, made by the multitudinous horizons and the clean transparent warmth of sun and air.

The flowers alone remained pessimistic in the sheltered cup of our oasis. They were still the marigold or dandelion or some less usual variety of the same composite invention, and in spite of sun and grass and water their yellow heads and flat encircling leaves clung without a stem to the winter-sheltering earth. What made them renounce the freedom of a stem that bends to every breath and turns its owner's glance to every corner, and is a plant's nearest approach to gaiety? Aeons of struggle must have taught them. When the tanks moved into Czechoslovakia one could think of such yellow flowers.

South of the Helmand gorges

The Lipstick girl

Chaikhane on the Afghan road

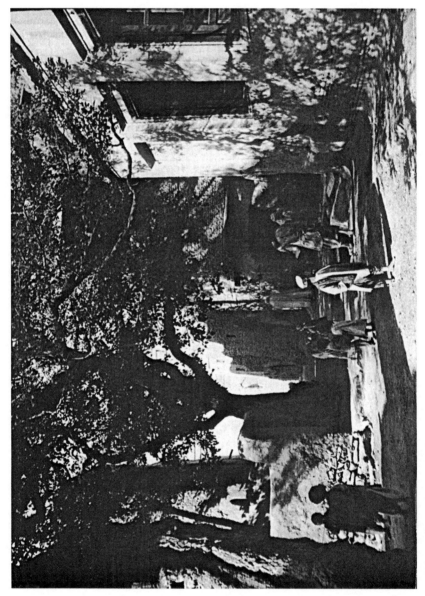

Afghan village

A higher downland spread just above. A man who came to squat beside us while we ate, with a three-cornered Mongolian face and eyes as light as the mountain sky, told us that their centre there is called Bâd-Asya, or Windmill; when we climbed to it we found three shops for a bazaar and a solidly built granary like those that Hadrian left along the Turkish coasts for his armies, with the same government look about it though in a smaller way. A shambling lorry trundled off down an unlikely track, and half a dozen people sitting at leisure to watch it gave a city touch, since agricultural leisure never begins in the morning. The country in the south descended in slopes of light or shadow towards clefts that led to Ghazni or the Kabul valley far away.

In this comparatively inhabited region the one-roomed houses had a mud wall squarely adjusted round mud domes, as if copied from the *yurts* of Central Asia. Larger groups, held together by an encircling wall, easily conjured up the camps of Chingiz or Tamerlane as the medieval missionaries or the Chinese travellers have described them, scaffoldings under domes and banners, with walls of silk, wool or brocade, where the royal wives walked under head-dresses so tall that they had to move into their tents backwards, and sat at the Khan's side at his banquets, and ruled the royal camps, each wife in her appointed place. The Mongol freedom and respect for women has died away, and nothing remains of the passing invasions except the tent-shape of these houses and the flattish faces of the Hazara descendants, in whose district we were travelling.

We drove on, over a wide and lovely movement of heights, from one corn basin to another, jade-green and translucent in their own depths of shadow, and slung as if suspended between fox-coloured slopes. The dust-road rounded them with edges vague as smoke, transitory and perpetual as the centuries of forgotten hooves that had trodden and bruised it into the background of its hills; and suddenly, without any preparation, we found ourselves on the brow of a precipice that looked down on Helmand escaping from its gorges. The river and a tributary met there, spitting white water and twisting like snakes surprised, and continued along an easier but still narrow valley journey, where a bridge at the bottom and the opposite zig-zags showed our way.

Our own side was the more precipitous. A lorry was clambering up, forward and back at every hairpin bend, while its passengers walked ahead in the white dust. Mark stopped to fill his pipe and look with some care at the prospect while still on the flattish top where wayfarers could cross, and when all was clear we too, slowly, took the corners never meant for anything longer than a mule from prow to stern.

We lacked the wooden *chop* or wedge with which every Afghan lorry goes provided: 'We must, we *must* get it,' said Claire, 'at the very next bazaar,' which was just a manner of speaking, for the landscape at that moment showed not a sign of habitation over all its vast horizons.

There were, however, plenty of stones. Zalmia kept one ready under his armpit and Francis now showed that surprising masculine characteristic which, however regardless of people, is selflessly devoted to machines; with an excellent eye he calculated exactly where the hillside might be expected to crumble, and the Land-Rover followed with cautious obedient grinding. The bridge at the bottom had been psychologically built of solid stone for reassurance, unlike the usual cantilever that, when its time comes, likes to die with a lorry in its arms.

It was noon and we had planned a rest, but the pit of the gorges was hot as a furnace and we swung gladly up again to the wind-visited heights; until they too got involved in western spurs and long straight shaly valleys with hamlets puny and farspaced between barren stretches of thorns and stones.

A gipsy girl, a *Kuchi*, eighteen years old perhaps, with a small morose son beside her, stood under a ruined tower in the most lonely place. She said that she owned a small garden up a side valley, and would like to go with us wherever we were going. Pretty and gay and pagan, with not a Puritan touch about her except possibly the puny Nemesis child, and dressed in the statuesque draperies that the Hellenistic carvings first recorded, she stood ready for anyone to pick her off the wayside. There was a little chaff with Zalmia, and 'We cannot take you,' we explained; 'but is there anything you need that you would like us to give?'

'Yes,' said she: 'A lipstick – red for the lips.'

About 5 p.m., after long descents through a network of worm-like rivers, the land grew kind again, the valley sides receded, and trees and grass appeared; and Panjau, the Five-Waters, a miniature village-town with some signs of coquetry about it, appeared with a sound of small cataracts among poplars, where the openings of the valleys made a natural resort.

The inhabitants of a minute bazaar gathered to point out the police fort, red and square mud with many mostly empty rooms inside it. A sub-commandant, roused from his after-noon sleep in a pair of very fine pyjamas, appeared to offer us a drawing-room and a meal. All we asked was a modest place to change in and the inner fortress court for the Land-Rover to camp. The Psychologist's party had not arrived when our sup-per was over; the moon was high already, the poplars swished and whispered beneath it round the rectangle of the court; and we were too tired to do more than notice a dim hum of conversation when the other party settled in an opposite corner some time during the quiet of the night.

4

Heroism and Tradition

A subdued coming and going occupied the police fortress of Panjau: young westernized students or clerks ran up and down to offices, and older citizens met each other sedately, their long-sleeved coats over their shoulders, while they talked in low voices and looked away discreetly from where our Land-Rover was settling for the night.

One of them, however, came up to me and inquired if the Police Commandant could ask for some medical advice as he was ill. He presently drew near – a worn, elderly and dignified man in what looked like a dressing-gown – and whether it was illness or shadow, the night seemed to have collected round his eyes in the dusk.

The Afghani is so like the Persian that, little as I remember of that language, it was enough to understand how our elementary help could be of no use to the Commandant, as the trouble was at his heart. 'But there is a doctor coming to camp tonight, and tomorrow morning before we leave I will interpret for you,' I said.

I did so just before we started while the other party, surrounded by the richest gadgets, were preparing to spend an easy morning before catching up with our next camp later in the day. It was a poor hour to introduce a stranger, even though we had been his guests in his court.

'I don't enjoy giving advice before breakfast,' said the irritated Psychologist, feeling the elderly pulse without any bedside manner. 'Tell him to come in an hour and I will give him some pills.'

The pretty secretary had discarded her mini-skirt and travelled in tactful blue trousers, and was now issuing from her camp-bed in a sleeveless silk pyjama that made her look slim as a water lily opening to the sun. She filled so much of the foreground that it was difficult for the Commandant to assume her to be invisible as he would have wished to do, being a well-bred man. But he understood the Psychologist's tone well enough, and remained dignified and quiet while I tried unsuccessfully to explain that pills would take an hour to prepare. Coming away, feeling like a prodded sea-anemone that shrinks round all its edges with annoyance, 'here we are,' I thought, 'losers of a world in less than three generations, and these are the manners that have lost it. Why on earth do people go on behaving like this *now* with nothing to be egocentric about any longer?'

Our Land-Rover was a refuge from such thoughts, and I persuaded Claire to share the front seat with me, although at the back it was no longer one of those old-fashioned prisons, and was everywhere excellent for seeing. But we could now converse as we travelled, and I understood her more clearly as she told me her story – an undefeated little figure, with a certain sober innocence compounded of optimism and goodness and sound Scotch sense all pouring together as from a cornucopia, intermingled. Everything living was enjoyment and grist to her mill.

She had been ill for eight, as I had for three, years: we both knew the emancipated feeling of a world whose fountains had so nearly closed; we knew too that the clear water can dry at any moment as one drinks it. A sense of fragility has been with me ever since – the cause of it now nearly sixty years ago: with her it had just happened, and she was intoxicated with life, its warmth, its adventure, its rough wear, all that it embraces. Her health was still far from secure, and we both, as a matter of fact, were more or less debarred from eating during a day or two; it made no difference; she was the best companion one could wish for.

Both she and Mark incidentally brought to life ideas which had been running in my head for some time, and which a particular quality of theirs seemed to confirm – a quality of reliance on principles which no pressure except persuasion could ever make them abdicate or yield. It was the strength that consoled my generation during many dark years, under Mediterranean 'resistance' or desert or English war, and was, indeed, *heroism*, the queen of virtues, not obvious and active here but latent, subtly pervasive, a climate of authority of which they themselves were unaware.

It is an almost unmentionable virtue at this time, chiefly from having been so long entangled with warfare, so that the people who should have been the natural heroes of a younger generation are overlooked or discarded and the perennial need for heroism in ordinary life is unrecognized. Yet the heroic is heroic in itself, independent of the casual vestures of its time. In my years it walked with familiar friendship through our streets and spoke to many a saddened heart: it stood behind the miracle of our improbable greatness of empire from its birth, and saw two oceans open and three continents secure for nearly a hundred years. No religion has established itself without it, nor should any aspirant press without its armour into whatever his private abyss of love or beauty may be. It is what no government, whether material or spiritual, can afford to miss since, from highest to lowest, heroism is the indispensable foundation for all rule, whether of oneself or others. It turns life into a symbol beyond the need of living; and grants fortitude and calm in exchange for the mere husk of human existence, when the necessity befalls. Without it, nothing worth remembering is achieved.

Yet because it is usually undisclosed, exhibiting itself rarely and carrying its solidity like an iceberg out of sight, it gets little recognition until it becomes manifest in action. It then appears, not of its own free will but propelled by some impulse or agent strong enough to screw the heroic with all its renunciations into the unwilling prose of life.

Nationalism, religion, philanthropy, adventure, or the threat or actual presence of intolerable anguish, may draw this power from its retreat; all have at one time or another set the heroic on its course. Yet these are themselves not more than façades, historically speaking – fashions inhabited and animated by whatever tradition is peculiar to each people.

Tradition is the profound and durable influence which directs the future from its past, and appears to be static and is not.

Its apparent immobility is that of the gun to the bullet, of
a bow to an arrow, or perhaps the vast push of earth to her
seed – the cradle whose dynamic nature is only shown by what
it generates. When the unity of such direction is interfered
with, the whole nature of a nation may change, as we are
constantly seeing in pressures of East and West; and when the
impulse behind action is divided, all heroic possibilities are
killed. The changes in tradition must come, but they should
be carefully guarded – from worse to better, but never from
better to worse.

'No man is able to make progress when facing two ways,'
says Epictetus; and that is what one is apt to do, from birth to
death, between one world and the other. 'One can't be sure
of *oneself*,' I find the nostalgic little entry in my diary . . . 'of a
lot of things, but not of oneself: the X in life is what one must
feel sure of.'

The hero pledges his all to the X in life and faces one way
only, whatever his station may be in peace or war; and the
power that gives him this direction is the tradition that has
suckled him, following its devious track through spirit and
blood and brain. From this opening as through a window he
sees and enters his universe; and strangely enough it does not
seem to matter whether his striving there is with or against the
stream: he is in his own ocean, swimming as he likes, and the
cross-current is often the most passionately guided to scour
its own substance against its own decay.

Some civilizations have been so generous in their nobility –
Greek, Roman, French, English at times – that they have
been able to throw a spell beyond their borders and make
alien heroes feel at home; more often the one tramples on the
other, snuffs out its altar candles, and leaves it in the dark:
yet even so, if its light was true, it may wait unrecognized for
ages and find another birth. But the fortunate civilizations are

Panjau to Chahcheran

Panjau to Chahcheran: Shahristan

The two gipsies

The way to Bend-i-Amir

those that follow their own spoke along the wheel of Time and move through ever-widening perimeters to their own portion of the general horizon: their tradition – like every tradition good or bad – is never static, but through every necessary deviation will keep its own direction – the arrow from the bow; and in the magnanimity which this world requires, will continue to produce the hero with indispensable care. For his is the quality which in the Arab horse is known as 'the enduring heart', essential for free survival. It is, I believe, the strongest force known in human life – the only one that can perhaps stand up to the atomic age.

My long digression comes back to Mark and Claire, in whose presence the English and Scottish traditions showed their basic reassuring complexion: our Land-Rover might have met Wilberforce, or Livingstone, or Nash the unfortunate traveller, or Walter Raleigh on his way to El Dorado, and all the Elizabethans in a bunch. Other sorts too – Ruskin collecting stones and flowers, Dr Johnson and even Boswell beside him, for the heroic range is very wide. We would have found ourselves at home with them, still talking the same language, enjoying the same humour, still able to combine – perhaps not quite so readily – obedience with initiative, following bureaucracy to the edge of its precipice but not beyond. Best of all, Chaucer and his pilgrims might have come riding over the Afghan uplands, less surprising in the landscape than our Land-Rover, for we were back in the world of their time.

We were now dipping in and out of shallow passes where the Helmand tributaries run south, while our way turned gradually northward to cut across the lowest spurs of Kuh-i-Baba, towards the waters of the Hari Rud.

We were skirting friendly green basins, treeless but filled with corn, with the myriad footprints of the nomads and their animals on the outer edge where the dry slopes began.

Down their steep curves, pitted with spiky cushions of the
acantholimon, white streaks appeared too perpendicular even
for an Afghan path, and I seem to remember that some traveller
has described these as land-slides for the bundles of winter
firewood which that unattractive little plant has to provide.
It marches over the barren hills like an army of hedgehogs
following the flocks, and indeed the *igelsteppe* where it grows
has been named after the hedgehog. Bulbs grow in the shelter
of its thorns, and at this time in August it was trying to push out
anaemic flowers of its own. It was stacked on the flat roofs in
bundles together with wild rhubarb, that makes large yellow-
leaved patches on the hills, and this winter storage seemed to
me very insufficient, but no doubt there was time before the
summer closed. The corn up here was still green, unlike the
lower valleys, and ran in geometric patterns of careful labour
up the hillsides wherever a *juy* looked substantial, as high and
even higher than its actual irrigation could reach.

Villages were sometimes little more than three or four
houses together, no longer domed in the *yurt* shape, but enclosed in blank mud walls and high-built almost windowless
corner-towers. A little latrine at the topmost corner gave
them a Gothic look of fortification, not unfamiliar to someone
brought up as I was on medieval romances. Smaller watch-
towers, many now ruined, stood on opposing slopes at the
beginning and end of the cultivated hollows that probably were
once separate jurisdictions. The sinews of Kuh-i-Baba pushed
barren arms among them and made one feel the smallness of
human enclosure and the greatness of distance, where anything might leap up unawares. We never met a car here, nor
many horses, but peasants riding home on black oxen loaded
with the produce of their fields on which they lived. Centuries
ago, when these routes were as easy as any others, the side-
stream of the oriental traffic must have flowed through them,

enjoying their jigsaw patterns of comparative safety, with tolls no doubt at the foot of every tower.

As we climbed towards the watershed the landscape opened to a moon-like naked pasture gently rising, with nomad horses grazing here and there. It was the Hari Rud watershed as a matter of fact, but looked as if it stretched flatly, with alongside a fringe of dark red rock scooped by weather into figure-clusters as like as anything in nature to Indian temple slopes. Here, above the valleys, the thin waters that trickled by would quickly dry when the last snow had melted above them.

In this uneventful waste where even the Land-Rover felt jaded, two women talked to us for a few minutes, walking out of nowhere side by side. They had become ageless, yet their hands had kept fine through their nomad years, and their faces beautiful with a majesty more permanent and rock-like than that of the average human face. Merely because they had met life out of its poverty and hardness this beauty had come upon them, as they walked at their own pace towards their shadows, in the tradition of their kin: and what do we give, I wondered, to these old sorrows of Africa or Asia that is not second-rate by comparison? The prize still goes to the 'enduring heart'.

We had crossed the watershed, and were making through less lonely country for a village grouped round a ruined castle which my map called Lal-i-Jangal. An excited crowd had gathered there to see a bus starting down the road we were to follow – which continued to be single in the landscape – and to watch us and the other party also, who now overtook and soon left us sitting at our tea on the café floor.

We followed through dull and thirsty defiles, till a new river-landscape opened before us, at about 3.30 in the afternoon. Our party was there looking doubtfully at some fish in the shadow of the bank – too small, they thought, and decided to drive on till river and fish grew bigger lower down: we would meet, they said, along the Hari Rud, of which this was a tributary stream.

It was called Sar-i-Jangal (Forest Head), and on its smooth banks, treeless in spite of its name, we spent the afternoon and evening, with thousands of grasshoppers whose singing fell suddenly silent as the sun went down. The only lorry we had seen since we left Lal, resting on every hilltop as we passed it, now swept by with a flourish along the downhill road; the last sparkle died on the bended arm of the stream, and the easy summits that surrounded us seemed to move away towards their nightly stations. The place sank into its houseless solitude, no more lonely than most solitudes in Asia – for a man soon turned up to ask if we had a cure for rheumatism and went away hugging a harmless little tube; he and a company of travellers, he said, were spending the night in a cave near by to catch the weekly bus for Lal which might or might not be passing next morning.

A young Swiss couple in a Land-Rover appeared and swerved on to our turf, drawn by its pastoral magic: they had done our journey in the opposite direction, and told us that we had only one truly difficult stretch and one really bad corner to deal with; they were abroad on their second honeymoon, a year in the world's freedom.

A very small boy came to drive away the black cows grazing at a distance. Air and water and the busy grass fell silent. In the thickening velvet of the night the moon was soon climbing her steep invisible stair.

5

Landscape in Asia

A trilling of birds greeted the sun.
It was early, but broad day and the world awake. A bee-eater, flying slowly upstream almost at water level watched, with rather the same expression as that of the Psychologist and his party the night before, the transparent grey battalions of minute fish steering against the current of their home.

The bus must have come and gone, for the travellers' cave was empty, with nothing left but some smouldering embers of their fire. The Swiss in their honeymoon caravan were still asleep; and the sun seemed to be enjoying his leisure before the business of the day began, splashing the yellow light of Persian dawns over the grassy hills, as if this shallow basin were his bath. A scene almost untroubled by human interference lay there relaxed in the cool hands of the solar hours, who would turn it gently round towards the west.

I have often wondered what catches us so sharply in the landscapes of Asia. They are hardly ever as beautiful as ours. There is no Afghan plain that I have seen as lovely as the Thames valley from Cliveden woods, no mountains rising as serenely perfect as Alps from their pastures; and yet prospects innumerable in all these Eastern lands, held for a few hours, or even moments, are never forgotten. It is a matter of size perhaps – what the ancient peoples felt obscurely when they carved their human figures so much smaller than their gods (wives, incidentally, only knee-deep to the Pharaohs). The atmosphere in the Asiatic landscape is not normal to us, its disproportion with the human figure is too vast, and the Hindu Kush soaring behind some tiny gathering makes us feel our own mortality as well as the immortal all about us. What we know, too, is added to what we see: the landscape that in Europe ends with North Sea or Mediterranean just over the brow of a hill, here stretches along the great silk road to China, with names of wayside halts that have accumulated magic through the ages, Louland or Khotan, Samarkand, Bukhara whose minaret – from whose parapet the condemned were thrown to destruction – held a light for travellers drifting in from the Red Sands, or passing on their way through Gobi to reach the Gates of Jade.

Names merely, you will say, but such as the pearl-master works on, encrusting its shred of grit with light; and it is this

recurrent sweep of distance and time, strokes of days unconsciously recorded, unconsciously noted, stray travellers' or
poets' words thrown casually, which like the jeweller's ham-
mer beat out the jewel's unnumbered facets into some lonely
but complicated climax of perfection – not landscape only,
but Time and Change, rise and decline of nations, all welded
into the traveller's moment as he passes, enriched beyond his
stride.

This, one may observe, is visible anywhere and could be
seen every morning as one walks to one's office, since time
and space are fluid along Thames as along Euphrates, and
everything one looks at is transition. But such basic facts are
what the human race, as soon as it has any initiative at all,
pathetically smothers out of sight. There is Fear beyond our
manageable span, and not an airline in the world but will offer
a *Sketch* or its equivalent to its passengers, trying to make their
atmosphere as like a dentist's waiting-room as possible to
save them from the dominant awareness of Pegasus or Orion
trotting so close beside them through the night.

Asia is no better than Europe or America in this respect and
will reduce its landscapes to the human level as soon as it has
the wealth or the leisure to do so; already new motels have
marigolds blossoming a 'Welcome' along the most beautiful,
Turkish, coastline of the world.

But Afghanistan at its centre is still inviolate. Seen from
the air, it looks unfit for habitation, its ribbons of water and
cuplike basins invisible in claws of rock that hold them under
the petrified ruffled feathers of their ridges. Even the emperor
Babur, in a very tough age, thought it remarkable to cross
these ranges, whose summer paths are tilted like ladders and
whose winters lie empty under snow. 'Such suffering and
hardship,' he says, 'as I have scarcely endured at any other

time,' and wrote a poem about it on the spot, likely to be his last.

'For about a week I helped in trampling the snow . . . Each step we sank to the waist or breast . . . and after a few paces a man became exhausted and another took his place. They dragged forward a horse without a rider; it sank to the stirrups and girths, and after advancing ten or twelve paces was worn out . . . In three or four days we reached a cave . . . at the foot of the Zirrin Pass [the Zard Sang, or Yellow Stone, between the two highest peaks of Kuh-i-Baba, 4697 and 5143 metres high]; the storm was at its worst . . . and the days were at the shortest. The troops began to arrive at the cave while it was yet light; when it was dark they stopped; each man had to dismount and halt where he was; many waited for morning in their saddles.

'I took a hoe and . . . made a resting-place for myself as big as a prayer carpet near the mouth of the cave; I dug down, breast deep, but did not reach the ground . . . They begged me to go inside, but I would not . . . whatever my men had to undergo, it was right that I should share . . . There is a Persian proverb that "in the company of friends death is a feast". By the time of the bed-time prayer the snow fell so fast that, as I had been all the time sitting crouched on my feet, I found four inches of snow on my head, lips and ears; that night I caught cold in the ear. Just then a party that had explored the cave brought word that it was very capacious . . . and I shook off the snow from my head and face . . . and sent to call those who were at hand. A comfortable place was found for fifty or sixty; those who had any eatables brought them out; and so we escaped . . . ' When they looked out next morning, the snow had stopped; and though many lost their hands or feet from frost-bite, they managed to climb the pass and reach the lower

The bridge south-west of Chahcheran

The first yurts and the young wife

The yurts *of Ahengari*

Shahrak to Djam

villages on the slopes we had looked up to on Kuh-i-Baba from the south.

Apart from the nomads, who travel to their pastures by tracks well-known in their seasons, and the gipsies or *Kuchis* who wander here and there, most women would hardly leave their village in a lifetime, nor would they clamber about the shaly slopes above it except perhaps for a gathering of the wild rhubarb now and then. Their flat-roofed houses, built of the earth that feeds them living and buries them dead, are safety incarnate, things their men will fight for in the uncertain world. Surrounded by fruit trees, or perhaps with a walled garden of apricot and mulberry near by, and with their threshing-floor close at hand, *immensity* of some sort, desert or mountain, broods around them with its brighter suns and darker shadows and different air – a presence pervasive but un-domestic to their ways. From such safety a man wanders and welcomes it as he returns; and grows up with it as the influence and yardstick of his being; and even to the casual visitor the sight of the small village will inspire tenderness, as of something unequally matched with the infinite.

This is still the general landscape of Asia, and we are liable to forget how deeply it must sink into a nation's earliest years. It existed in the West, in a smaller measure, and in my childhood on the sparsely inhabited outskirts of Dartmoor I can remember the same sort of sensation of safety as one turned in at one's own gate of the home field, and even more so the island feeling of a few small farms (destroyed in 1943, when the neighbourhood was considered suitable for training the U. S. armies in the grimness of war). Left out beyond anything but a heathery cart track, with the loneliness of the moors around them, their weathered gates and troughs and bright ploughs and milk pails were so many symbols of

human life set in the brave but unequal proportion of their
background.

Ever since the tower of Babel was built in the first adventure against space, people have been aware at intervals of
the supremacy of Man. It remains perhaps to be proved, but
meanwhile the landscape of our age advertises it, regretfully
but with success, pushing the more permanent background
out of sight. The mountains are there, but the factories take the
foreground, and the seaside villa intrudes before the sea; and
it is only in untamed corners that one can forget – or possibly
remember – to whom the world belongs. The 'underdeveloped* countries' (the arrogance of this term was almost
incredible) – these poor underdeveloped countries may con-
sole themselves with the reflection that no great religion was
ever born in a landscape whose foregrounds are completely
occupied by man.

We were now travelling from our ridges and uplands towards shallower depressions, by easy passes from cultivation
to solitude and down again to cultivation, with the double
watch-towers still guarding every inhabited valley. In a lower
dip than usual, by a small river, some local potentate of the
past had left a bridge; it was roughly built, of stone with a
band of brick-work at the arches, with four rather amateur
whitewashed columns, two at each end; the road was good
here, with cultivation lower down, and a laden donkey was
passing by now and then, or a cart or – more surprisingly –
a jeep-load of Peace girls who were spending two years in
this remote corner; the valley otherwise held only trees and
water, and sheep led down to drink before their long day's

---

* A few years ago someone noticed the tactlessness of this adjective and sub-
  stituted 'developing', which leaves one with the interesting impression that
  while they are striding on, the rest of us are not developing at all!

browsing in the sun; and the bridge with its ornament – so unique in this country – appeared as the pastoral throne of the valley, that Lycidas or Daphnis might have seen.

Over the next pass we first met the *yurts* of Central Asia, circular tents with walls of wooden slats or reeds, inherited from the Mongols. From now on they would alternate with the lopsided black tents of Arabia, the 'houses of hair'. This particular camp was poor and untidily perched down a slope, and looked as if some wind had tossed it there, as fragile as foam on the breast of a wave. Its women came out to Claire and me, astonished but ready to be friendly, though their language was Pashtu, and therefore unintelligible to us; but they were pleased to be photographed, and the young wife only half hid while we were posing her; when the master of the camp came along and took the situation in hand, she disappeared to her own tent where he presently followed, and evidently slapped her, for she came out holding her cheek and weeping loudly, while he continued to talk Afghani politely.

We were now well down towards the drainage of the Hari Rud, and our mountain atmosphere was changing. The flowers were different; misty blue drifts of chickory appeared; eremurus, convolvulus pink or white, artemisia and blue and yellow daisies, and others unknown. A broad and shallow valley spread with lion-coloured cliffs, and the Hari Rud – turquoise transparent water – flowed broken over slabs of yellow stone. The Herat wind was blowing dust, and all was a white dazzle in the sun. The road ran straight, used by lorries, though all we saw were riders here and there; we were on the horse-loving side of the watershed.

As we drove along, a man stepped out towards us from a garden, and we saw through his weatherbeaten clothes and scorched face that he was a fair youngish man – American, he said. He had a hired horse drooping under an almond tree behind him, and was riding from Herat to Kabul by easy stages; he had been wandering for three years and was happy. Few people tell one that they are happy! We asked if he had all he needed? Did he find food? Did he know the language? Was there anything we could supply?

'No,' said he, beaming up at us with his burnt face and eyes almost shrunk away with dust and sun: 'I need nothing; I have everything; it's fine; I just came out to say good morning.' We left him, 'trusting in God', he said, and foolishly never asked what first made him take to his road; and have been wondering ever since.

Chahcheran (which our other map calls Qala Qausi) is the chief centre along this route, and was important to us as the only place where petrol was to be found. Even that was not very certain, and there was a further question of how to carry enough to take us on over the most difficult stretch of our journey. This problem, as practically every other one in Turkey, Persia and Afghanistan (not always quite so much in Arabia), should be taken by a sensible person to the police; and it was particularly advisable in the Afghan mountains where there was no one else to go to.

Asia invented the turquoise dome to shine through the haze and conquer, but the attempt is no longer made in utility villages like Chahcheran: new rectangular houses sat on the valley's flatness under lashing dust, that nibbled walls and corners of cement as it had once devoured the softer fancies of many forgotten dynasties. We reached it at the merciless zenith of noon and found an aggrieved note from the Psychologist complaining of the perennial wind which he called a sandstorm and telling us that they had gone on. We stopped at a low-roofed police hut to ask help for our petrol, and said we would call on the Commandant at a more reasonable hour.

A policeman came with us to where a gold-embroidered skull-cap and immaculate turban squatted in the dust ready to pour petrol from iron barrels in the open; and Zalmia and the police went off to see how many empty five-gallon tins could be found to lay flat under our bedding on the Land-Rover's roof. We waited meanwhile in the bazaar tea-house, cross-legged on carpets, discussing our route with a travelling merchant, and smiled upon by the pin-up beauties plastered round the walls. It was a gloomy twilight place, with no screen of trees in front or veranda roofed with matting where one might sit out of the sun in the open; the whole row of progressive little shops, punctured with black doorways like eyes without eyelashes, was naked to dust and sunlight.

As we left the town we called on the Commandant, and found him trimly uniformed, polite and cheerful in an office even more uncompromisingly bare than the bazaar. He had been telephoning about our road, and advised us to abandon it and make south for Kandahar, and we had to describe the whole history of the minaret of Djam and its artistic importance before we could persuade him to contemplate our going. But when we talked of our pleasure in sleeping out among the hills he melted: he looked after his district on horseback and knew its smallest pathway. "Look out," said he, "for a spring of delicious water with trees beside it, when you reach the other slope of the pass."

The afternoon was getting on, but we hoped to climb out of the wind before dark, and left the Hari Rud where it plunged into its gorges. We crossed an open plain of grass that might have been a village common, only wider, where a colony of well-to-do *yurts* had scattered their painted tent-walls and carved doors. The place was called Sar-i-Ahangaran (the Blacksmith's Head) and still had a settled air about it, with a clump of trees too far off to visit and what looked like

ruined houses on a rise. It could be some old country church
in England in the evening light, with its shade and gravestones
round it: but in fact it had been the capital of the Ghurid
Shahsabanis, who gave trouble to Sultan Mahmud of Ghazni,
and had three expeditions (at least) sent against them, and
were defeated in the eleventh century (A.D. 1011). Sultan
Mahmud kept his enemy's son as a vassal, and left him teachers
to instruct his people in the tenets of Islam; and the little state
continued to flourish together with the brothers and uncles
and cousins who carved out their separate jurisdictions and
made up the Ghurid clan. They finally stepped into the shoes of
Ghazni, until the Mongol invasions swallowed all: but before
this, the Ghurid tribute, when it was sent along the defiles,
would include not only fierce dogs, but coats of mail and
armour – local products which surely had some connection
with the blacksmith name of Ahangaran that has survived?

The evening was falling, and we began to climb, looping
south-west to avoid the gorges; we hoped to cross the pass and
find the Commandant's oasis before dark. But the track grew
worse and the pass receded, and we camped before nightfall
by the highest trickle of water we were likely to find.

6

The Herat Wind

As a guest in the Land-Rover, and because its routine was long tried-out and excellent, it never occurred to me to make suggestions except in the matter of water. There, I felt, Claire's discrimination failed her and optimism won: she would look at the *juy* dancing along its carefully tilted channel in débutante purity, and refuse to believe that there were tents round the hidden corner where *everything* found

its way into the stream. Flowing water is almost a religion
in the remoter lands of Persia. It is held to purify what it
touches, and I believed Afghanistan to be the same – very
unlike Turkey, where drinking is a matter for connoisseurs.
We therefore took to stopping near anything insignificant
enough to be pure, and filled our cans with it as it trickled
from the heart of its own hills; and this evening we camped
by the smallest drip that we met on the whole of our journey.
At times it disappeared altogether, or could only be traced by
steep green blotches among the stones.

It was a poor place: two slopes of boulders and the voiceless
thread of water, and nothing else except a lozenge of sky cut
by the mountain sides. The moon, touched with age, looked
pinched as she crossed over, and a thin wind came nosing like
a hound up the cleft of our ascent. Where there is so little to
look at the visual mind is at rest, the imagination can wander;
in the high air so clear of vegetation one could think of the
earth like a white dove tumbling in the darkness of the sky.
I fell asleep on this remote panorama, and only woke as the
numbed figures of my companions began to shed a few extra
mufflers in the first touch of sun.

The Commandant's paradise was promised on the far side
of the pass and we were anxious to breakfast lower down
beside it: the pass led us on, it reached one rounded top after
another, dry hills of shale, flat slabs of limestone, and tufts of
the hedgehog *acantholimon* – and here and there below us the
green reluctant patches that slowly grow to streams. Far to the
right we dismissed a clump of small trees, forgetting how easily
the humble East is pleased with trees and water; and we saw
nothing else that the Commandant might have liked to sit and
rest by. We ran down a long low snout into the lowlands, and
the dust engulfed us – the Herat wind was blowing from the
west. It does this, they say, for 120 days through the summer.
When we reached the Ishlan valley, which runs south of the

The North Afghan horse

Chaikhane on the Afghan road

Hari Rud and almost parallel with it until they join, the dust was racing towards us like a train. It squeezed through the footboards and rolled in waves behind us, clearing now and then to show a rag of sky above. The valley was broad and flat, and the Ishlan ran small down the middle of it between rudiments of cliff set in the wrong direction, pipes for the wind: the valley sides sank in low peninsulas like paws, too smooth for protection; the wind and dust rolled about them as if they were kittens to play with.

We were hungry for our breakfast and scattered here and there to find some crease of shelter and, having crossed a small arm of the river to look at its cliffs, and given my exquisite Maxwell shoes their first wetting, I would have found it unmanageable to walk back against the blast if Mark with his habitual gentleness had not thought of walking downstream to see me safe across.

The pleasure of the morning was a rider on his horse with a man on foot behind him, descending among the swirl of the dust as if a part of the tossing landscape had somehow got itself detached and were returning. On the grassy or sandy stretches north and west of the Afghan ridges the horses were always a delight to meet. Their Arab kinship shows in the ears which are quaintly pointed with a little hook towards each other; but the general build, although just as small, is more solid and the head longer, and the chest not quite so bold in curve; the Tang horse in my study is very like them. They are strong like their cavaliers, who sit squat in the saddle with curved and rounded shoulders whenever they mean business in their riding. The horses are loved and petted and brought up together with the family in the tents; and the young foal on which his owner's hopes are set will walk with delicate steps unburdened, secure of attention and everybody's care.

Our rider's path came close to where we stood. We called to him to stop so that Claire could take a picture, and he caracoled to and fro regardless of the wind, pleased to show what he and his mount could do.

By this time we had given up any thought of a rest in the arena of the Ishlan valley, and pushed downstream over a low headland round a defile that could have been sheltered if it had been turned the other way: as it was, we knew the wind would be blowing through it like a triton through his horn, and skirted it on our left; and coming on to lower ground on the farther side, found that the headland itself gave reasonable protection to a wide dip where river and sheep could browse together among bushes and sand. On the far side, in bright sunlight and beyond a ford which we crossed, was the Rabat of Pam.

This word, *rabat*, can be found scattered over frontier districts of the Muslim world wherever their conquests were sufficiently hindered to require fortified places and time. Its root, in my Arabic dictionary, branches into fifteen separate meanings: to tie, to be resolute, to menace a frontier, to be entangled or make an agreement, to be brave, or a bundle, or a highway robber, an inn or hospice, a rope or chain, a binding stone in a building, a monk, an enclosure or a stable, or a halter; this fascinating variety, all swelling from the same root, would lead one into philology if one had the time. As it is, it makes the charm of the Arabic language, where the family relationships of words are particularly obvious and show the mental processes behind them that deal for instance with the *idea* of enclosure and make monk and stable and agreement and entanglement all coalesce together.

The *rabat* began as a frontier post entrusted to dedicated warriors who lived in confraternities not unlike the Templars and Knights of St John in a later age. The most splendid castles of these fighting colonies are those along the Tunisian coast at Sousse, Monastir, and Minia, hewn in stone; but they exist along the Afghan caravan tracks also, built, as it seemed to me, at distances of a day's ride one from the other, and all of the same pattern – a wide mud-walled square with a roughly ornamented gateway at the centre of one side, and a small mosque in the middle of the open space; the travellers' rooms, with a portico for his animals and baggage, ran all around the inside of the square. A peculiarity which I had not noticed anywhere else were troughs for horses' fodder scooped in the outside mud of the enclosing wall. Most of these edifices, built of mud like the village houses and towers, have fallen into shapeless heaps, and the *rabat* of Pam was no exception; it must have been re-erected many times since the first guard was set on the river-crossing and the good grazing around it, in the border wars that leave no history but legend.

They went on through the eighth and ninth centuries AD, and long after in many districts where Muslim spearheads continued to push their way into the plateaux of Central Asia. At Panjkent, in the oasis of Samarkand, the Russians are now excavating a site taken and burnt by Arab assailants, and frescoes rescued from the mounds of this destruction show the Persian fashions of a time before the Arabs came; they were dressed for peace and banquets along their walls, in fine brocaded gowns, but the round steel cap which appears with a spike on top, was armour, such as the ancestors of our *rabat* must often have watched coming and going across the ford.

We sheltered in the lee of its wall, out of the wind in the sun. It was still only a little after ten in the morning and a flock was being led to water at the river bend. After it had drunk, it arranged itself for the noonday heat individually under any poor scrap of shade that the bushes could offer, or collectively with heads all drooped towards the centre like a wheel, secure but stifling under the sun. It seemed sad that this remarkable example of collective effort should accomplish nothing but a small mitigation of the discomforts of life: even this, we rather gloomily reflected, seemed more than the human world can manage in our time.

Our road now climbed from the Ishlan into abrupt and rocky landscape mostly out of the wind, and brought us to the level of a north-westerly valley from which the way to the minaret of Djam branches northward, some six miles before the headquarters of the district are reached at Shahrak.

This is a poor little place where a police guide might be found. It had a rest-house belonging to the meteorologists, in a walled garden full of hollyhocks, poppies and petunias among quiet lorries; and a two-storeyed house for travellers in the middle. Two rooms for sitting or sleeping were on the upper story, carpeted with the red Bukharas general in this country, and a third was furnished with Western bedsteads, table and chairs. A young English doctor with a Burmese wife on their way to Thailand were asleep there.

The lorry drivers, squatting in comfort on the Bukhara carpets, filed out without a murmur on being told that we wanted to wash, since privacy (as far as the company of men is concerned) is one of the few privileges a *harim* is entitled to. By the time we were clean the doctor and his wife appeared – a delicate Burmese, pretty as a butterfly and pregnant with a four-month baby. The doctor was tall, with soft eyebrows and the brown embryo of a beard, and harassed at the moment by his Land-Rover which had come to grief on its way to Djam. Some vital part would have to be mended in Herat, and a week had gone by without a lorry either going or coming to take it there and back.

They were very young optimists, the wife perhaps less so, for timorous flute-like notes of anxiety came through in her melodious English now and then. The doctor had a job waiting in Bangkok, to be reached from Herat through Kandahar and over the Khyber pass, along the Great Trunk road through Pakistan and India and beyond – asphalt more or less all the way. Curiosity alone had pushed him here into the wilderness. He had an inquiring engaging mind, wandering easily into abstract byways where two and two make five and sometimes reach infinity, and he promised to come for a drink with us after sunset; by then he was in bed with dysentery and a high fever. We called in to see him, and heard he was no better next morning, and left him with a jar of Horlick's and a five-pound note which I carry about in case of accidents.

"You can't take it," said the Burmese wife to her husband imploringly. "We may never be able to pay it back." These fragile women! A thread of steel runs through them.

"You *must* take it," I said; "I have been ill too and left ever so many debts of kindness unrepaid. It is the only thing that makes the world totter along."

They took my address and some months later a cheque reached me from Lahore; the doctor had wandered again, to look at Hunza or Nepal while the wife was waiting for her baby and all was well. The letter had no address, so that I was unable to thank them, or to hear of them settled at last in Thailand, and flourishing, I hope.

The Police Commandant of Shahrak, whom we had called upon in his office, returned our visit in the course of an hour or two. He was a *sayyid* of the Quraish, the Prophet's tribe, originally from Mecca but settled for centuries in Kandahar, and his finely drawn profile was Persian rather than Afghan or Arab. So was the low and gentle voice in which he spoke to us; it remained low but became less gentle when he gave orders to his men. Now that we had crossed the watershed between Eastern and Western Afghanistan, the Persian influence became much more noticeable, even in language, so that anyone who knew the Afghans well would distinguish the speech of Kandahar or Herat or Kabul. The Commandant's three sons were also *sayyids* and addressed as such by the servant who looked after the smallest baby still in arms; fair-skinned, with grey-green eyes and easy manners, they were growing up loved and petted and accustomed to command in the day-to-day life of these outer districts where the rule of Governor or Police Commandant is absolute, however tight the rein may be drawn in Kabul.

The *sayyid* described the difficulties of his task – not so much the hardness of geography and climate that has to be faced on horseback, but the fact that modern laws often conflict with the age-old Afghan traditions which have been kneaded into the people's very bones. "They must constantly pay penalties for breaking laws of whose existence they are quite unaware," he said. "And that is the most distressing part of my work. The chief crime here is murder – not of strangers, who are well treated – but among themselves; and where justice has been a private affair, for ages carried out under well-established rules, they cannot understand why these rules should suddenly be turned into crimes against the law."

The Commandant spoke of his people with pleasant feeling and of the tradition which had been teasing my thoughts ever since we left Kabul. Here in the mountain valleys, so long cut off from the general highway, out of sight or contact with the changing world, it had not adapted itself, and *growth*, the most delicate of all traditional processes, had lain dormant and neglected. It was the Police Commandant's hard duty to bridge the gap that now yawned between the old and new. He was doing so with kindness and the changes would come the more easily as they settled more slowly; it would take a long time for the whole modern panorama to invade the rocky valleys of Shahrak.

When the Commandant left, our beds stood ready-made on a terrace in the rest-house garden, among lorries sufficiently road-worn in the moonlight to fit without too much of a shock into the medieval background of Afghanistan.

7

The Minaret

We were about to reach the climax of our journey. A day's travel and one mountain range only lay between us, from the level and rather dull bed of the Shahrak valley northwards, then almost due east over high downland ridges, and north again down a tributary gorge to where a bunch of precipices met. Here the Hari Rud swerved round the minaret in one of those alluringly dotted blue lines by which a map expresses the unsurveyed. The ridge we still had to cross showed a sort of saddle, steep on its northern slope, between the two highest points of the Safed Kuh, 3525 and 3416 metres respectively; and we could see its tossing and beautiful skyline before us as we turned from our valley.

The minaret stands alone and perfect, with no other building near it except an almost invisible scrap or two of castle ruined on a high scarp above. Its whole surface from top to bottom is covered with rectangles, lozenges, stars, knots and fancies of deep-cut tracery in the hard-baked earth which the Islamic art of the eleventh and twelfth centuries knew how to handle to such purpose: nothing has gone from it except the wooden balcony which must once have supported the *muezzin* when he called his call to prayer, and some of the bricks near the foundation which need to be replaced. The door too, which must once have given access to a double staircase of a hundred and eighty steps that interweave themselves inside, is now no more than a hole in the wall. Otherwise the whole slender structure stands as its builders saw it, eight centuries passing over it as over the Sleeping Beauty, with little except the rustle of the poplars and the voice of birds and water to disturb its sleep. An airman from Herat, wandering off his course in 1957, first saw its surprising shape at the meeting of four wild and stony gorges; and the inscription of Sultan Ghiyāth al-Dunya wa'l-Din Abu'l-Fath Muhammad b. Sām, fifth sultan of the Ghurid dynasty AD 1163–1203, is all of its history that is known.

This was the age before Chingiz Khan and his Mongols swept down with their destruction; and in its short span one civilization after another flowered from the Persian stem, rising and vanishing, rich and evanescent, in the Asiatic trade.

Minaret of Djam

Minaret of Djam: detail

The Providential guide

Top: Assisting the Land-Rover
Bottom: The ford of the Hari Rud

The Ghurids are particularly interesting because, almost alone in the great arena of Central Asia, they seem to have been essentially local both in their origins and in their later development. Eastern Iranian Tajiks, their language differed from the Persian of the court at Ghazni in the south, their religion did not begin to convert itself to Islam until the eleventh century, and their infantry – behind the tortoise wall of their shields – managed to defeat the elephants of Ghazni. When the greatness of Ghazni declined, the Ghurids took over, steering prudently round the growing Turkish powers and dividing the mountain principalities among the members of their family, as they fell to them one by one.

Firuzkuh, where the minaret remains,[*] was their capital for more than sixty years from the reign of Baha al-Din in A.D. 1149, until conquered in 1210, and finally destroyed by Chingiz in 1222. Before this happened, the dynasty had already been losing one province after another to the Khwarizm-Shahs who ruled beyond the Oxus and whose quarrel with Chingiz brought on the destruction of Central Asia and themselves.

In this catastrophe the Ghurids disappeared. But they had ruled from northern India to eastern Persian Khurasan, expanding westward from Firuzkuh and establishing a younger branch at Ghazni, after its conquest, to overflow into India down the perennial route of armies. They conquered Bamian and Balkh and the passes of the Oxus, into the highlands of Badakshan on the road to China; they were victorious at Merv and nominated governors as far as Nishapur in the west. The sultan who built the minaret died at the opening of the thirteenth century in his newly acquired city of Herat.

---

[*] According to A. Maricq and G. Wiet: *Le Minaret de Djam:* Mem. de la Délégation Archéol. Française en Afghanistan: XVI. Paris 1959. There is still some controversy as to the site.

Their own armies were infantry of the mountains, helped
by bodies of Turkish mercenary cavalry whose generals continued the military tradition of the Ghurids in Delhi long
after the overstretched empire had fallen and the last of their
sultans had been deposed in Firuzkuh. During this brief and
strange interlude, poets and architects and artists had flourished, and the Persian tradition had been treasured. In the
cities they conquered, new mosques and schools were built,
and the literature that fell into the sultans' hands was saved
and sometimes added to by poems of their own. It seems to
have been a Persian characteristic through the ages to preserve
what they could of the cultures they had done their best to
destroy.

We were now within a day's reach of this objective, with
a policeman to guide us and only one really bad corner to
negotiate, where a Belgian and his driver have since fallen
over and been killed. All experienced friends had warned us
of it until it turned into a sort of fable, the giant or Cerberus
or dragon who guards the enchanter's hold. Meanwhile, having left at 7.30, we turned off from yesterday's road into
an easy, watered valley filled with corn and willows, whose
very name of Spring-head (Sar-i-i-Cheshmé) spoke of old-
established comfort, however poor the village that remained.
It was half nomad with tents among the houses, and probably
abandoned at some seasons of the year; yet even so, set on
low ground where the spring water ran smooth as glass beside
it, with its mud hovels as perishable as any earthly habitation, its atmosphere was that of something permanent and
indestructible, the secret of water in a thirsty land.

Most of the Spring-head inhabitants were higher up, in a
long hollow free of crops and good for grazing. They owned
camels, which become much more frequent as one crosses

the ridges towards the Hari Rud; and while they sat about in groups, happy in their short summer and the shade and freshness of the morning, their animals wandered as they liked among the boulders, under two walls of cliff.

Our route was not meant for wheels, but had been cleared of rocks. Two of the camels stood in the middle of it, and looking at us from their aristocratic height and supercilious poise, recognized us for what we were – serfs of the machine, not free to wander – and stepped with nonchalant disdain to finish their conversation among the boulders. They paid no attention to an almost baby camel near them which had evidently never seen a Land-Rover before. It panicked on to the road in front of us and trotted desperately, too agitated to notice that safety lay all round to right and left; and we ought to have stopped altogether to let the crisis die down; but we made the mistake of driving very slowly and gently, while two children – 11 or 12 at most – came running up, clung to the baby's neck, pulled it in opposite directions, and added their puny strength to the disorder. Even a baby camel is strong, and this one shook its herdsmen off like fleas; keeping to the road with increased determination, it trotted along more quickly than before, its legs moving together, first one side then the other, with the absurd look of a rocking-horse rocking sideways instead of plunging fore and aft, and with its loose little hump tufted with baby curls nodding in a dishevelled way like the untidy chignon of a Toulouse-Lautrec barmaid. We kept at a good distance and expected it to stop; but the whole valley had evidently become anathema to it and our policeman explained that it would be making for its old camp, hours away through the defile.

This gloomy thought occurred to the two boys, who now separated and ran under the cliffs to head it off; with their moss-green draperies flying and their swift wide steps down

the steep from boulder to boulder, they looked like angelic
messengers descending through space rather than the incom-
petent little herdsmen we had seen them to be. We waited till
they were out of sight where the valley narrowed, for we knew
they would never get their camel to face us in a defile. When
we finally turned the corner, it had vanished long ago and the
two pursuers sat side by side on a rock waiting peacefully for
fate to intervene. This it did, for we offered to take them on
their way till the track turned off, and were just helping them
into the car when the sight of our policeman had the same
effect on them as the Land-Rover had on the camel, and if
they had not been firmly held they too would have escaped.
They were deposited, too surprised to be happy, at the turn
of the track, where a wider meeting of valleys allowed them
(and Zalmia) to head off the camel after all.

This adventure took up more of the morning than we had
intended, but we now made good going from one smooth
empty green bowl of a valley-head to another until, dipping
to a grassy stretch longer and flatter than usual, with a tree and
a house or two upon it, we saw the Psychologist's Land-Rover
with its muster grouped about it, already on its way home,
and stationary and shining in the sun.

The Psychologist's party should by rights have been the
villain of this story, since every story needs a villain of sorts
and there was none other available: and so they would have
been, if they had lived up to the Agatha Christie form of our
start and kept near enough for drama to have its chance. And
we had a grievance too, for we had been asked to wait for
them in Kabul and by so doing lost an added day or two
beside the minaret; and here we were being abandoned again
(not that we minded), close upon the difficult place where
breakages were expected to occur, while they put a mountain
range or two between us and swallowed the Afghan miles
like pills. Lord Halifax once told me of a cabinet minister

who was taken out hunting and got into trouble at a gate; and while fumbling at the catch turned to the stamping crowd behind him to say: 'Please remember, gentlemen, that we are doing this for enjoyment.' His words were surely wasted, as they would have been on our Psychologist, though Bill Allen's rather wistful battered look suggested that he might have enjoyed a pause in the minaret's shadow, talking of life under the Ghurids.

The ridge and its corner were steep enough, and the length of the Land-Rover had to be manœuvred on a two-way slant; the clayey soil full of small gritty pebbles would betray any weight upon it even after a minimum of rain: but no drop fell during the whole of our journey, the ground stayed hard and firm, and Francis came into his own with a rock under each arm and the knack of pushing it in before the mountain edge began to crumble. He and Zalmia ran forward and back, Mark sucked his pipe hard and carefully followed the signals, Claire and I watched full of suitable admiration, and in a surprisingly short time we were looking north from the highest pass of the Safed Kuh at ranges that hem in the Hari Rud.

The two highest summits were right and left of us, and we looked on to the tops of coloured mountains – a Russian salad of lobster pink, mauve, cream, a touch of jade – tangled between us and the river gorges. As we dipped down a steep slope towards them, a valley opened descending north-easterly along the Tagao Gombaz, an earth-coloured stream: what could it be but drab, with not a patch of grass among the rocks that fed it? But the valley itself, after a caterpillar course downhill, became gentle and splendid between precipices and summits; cornfields and trees appeared; old apricots and willows developed a forest beauty I had never seen; and two of the three villages of Djam showed themselves, climbing beside their *juys*, among fruit trees higher than the roofs of their houses.

This was a riding country, for nothing on wheels except a Land-Rover or a jeep would get along here, and a rider sitting on embroidered saddlebags met us on the narrow way that ran between hillside and water; he put his horse up the steep bank to let us by.

Not much in the village has probably changed since the days of the Ghurids, though their mosque portico seemed to remember better times in its simple decoration. The people looked as if they had kept the sturdiness that carried them so far in their day. They gathered about us, with bright, very sweet green apples, and yellow plums, and apricots which are spread at this time on all their roofs to dry; and their *mullah*, schoolmaster, talked to us while waiting for the *arbab* or headman of the village.

He was a fair-skinned young man, who read the Commandant's letter, offered tea, and bade us welcome; but, as it was well after noon, agreed to give us a guide at once to the minaret, some three miles down the stream. The valley turned north and grew narrow and steep below the village; the stream went gurgling down it with umber cliffs overhanging, and tamarisk, berberis, and such Mediterranean shrubs among its boulders. The lavender and eremurus spikes of the upper hills had disappeared; and we were in a warm habitable world where, the villagers told us, the winters have little snow.

At a corner between cliffs, the minaret was there, straight and tapering as a candle or a beautifully rolled umbrella, etched from top to bottom with patterns, ribands and bands and medallions, cut in the hard-baked brick whose biscuit colour showed light against the mountain walls. Almost under its octagonal base our little stream threw itself into the Hari Rud, that swept with loud green waters along its farther side.

Extraordinarily remote, without a house or a human being, the place seemed to be quivering with life: the river, the breeze, the brambles of wild roses, the trees and their shadows, the bits of castle wall that hung upon the rock across the water, the Past trampling through the defiles, and the minaret itself soaring into the sky with the impetus of its design still active upon it – a volume seemed shut there in a language no human key could open, a joyous strangeness whose natural laws we shared but could not understand. I have often come upon this feeling, breaking upon some torrent in uninhabited valleys, or secret sanctuary of the hills – the song of the world that goes on where man is not around; and always its huge exuberance fills me with a delight no human average reason can explain.

We had the afternoon hours to relax in. Francis took them actively and climbed the rather interrupted double staircase and the castle rock by its vanished gateway, where he found shards of pottery like that of Gurgan and of thirteenth-century Alamut, also destroyed by the Mongol armies. Mark stretched himself out to read in the slowly swinging minaret shadow, and Claire and I washed our clothes in the tributary stream and spread them on wild rose-boughs to dry.

As the light poured level down the western defile, I wandered upstream to find a place to bathe in, and discovered a small beach of fine sand under an arch of willows where the water was strong but not too steep, and lapped against cool rocks as finely veined, as smooth and firm as flesh. Just beyond this shelter it was creased like silk, and of a colour that seemed to bind the sky and forest with the light of their days inside them; and lower down it poured irresistible against rocky sides, until it broke to shallows that a child could ford (and we saw one do so). The path along the opposite bank, once the main way to Chahcheran through the defiles and loud with the Ghurid conquests, was so lonely that I took no account of it and undressed beside the pale rock, thinking of river legends when the world was young. Perhaps one then understood the language and gaiety of these solitary places and, as I laid my sophisticated underwear on the rock, a far-away day came into my mind when I too had met Daphnis in the hills.

This was on the island of Zant, and I was climbing Mount Scopas (I think that was the name) at 2 a.m. in order to see the sunrise. My friends sent me in a taxi to the bottom of the hill, where the driver pointed out a small darkling path which I followed without much trouble for something over an hour in the starlight, until the first gleam of morning began to show. I was near the top where a church stands and the path branches in two directions and, as I hesitated, a young shepherd appeared as it seemed out of nowhere in the half light (he was wearing the silent moccasins of the island). I had no Greek, and could only point and say, where?, and he led me first to the hilltop from which we watched the red streaks of the dawn and all the beauty, and then to the little church with its silver ikon for the yearly feast. I sat for some time looking at all these things, and he sat a little way off contemplating me, but as we came down towards our first meeting-place he drew near and took my arm very gently through his own. My rudiments of Greek happened to include the word *oxi*: if it had been *ne* (yes), the story might have become more complete: but I said *oxi* in a manner as smiling and as gentle as his own, and he vanished among the rosemary and arbutus as quietly as he had come.

He would have been a god, or at least a demi-god, in easier times; as it is, he has remained with me and the scents of the early morning through the years; and I thought of the little episode as I soaped myself all over and moved to step into the stream. The pale sand began to swallow my feet: oh dangerous river-gods! But the rock was of a convenient shape to hold, and I pulled out my feet already sucked to the ankles, and swung myself into deep water where the clear loveliness tugged over and round me with teasing ripples that meant no

The ruins of Chist: detail

The ruins of Chist

Harvest on the Hari Rud

Herat. The Mosque door

Herat. Gauhar Shad minaret

Herat. One of the four minarets

harm; until I climbed back with all the river coolness on me, over the rock on to firmer sand.

There is only a small area of flat green grass and cultivation round the minaret; the three defiles and the escarpments with which they end close it in on every side, so that there is always some shade except when the sun is plumb overhead at noon. One wonders where the capital city of Firuzkuh managed to bestow itself for there is practically no room and nothing is left to a casual search except the remnant of a tower across the tributary stream and a small low platform in the middle of the field. Lower down an old man told us he owned and lived in an apricot garden. He had a long white gown and silvery beard, and came to sit with us over our tea and ask for medicine for his eyes. This is the saddest thing they ask for, since one knows that nothing one can suggest will help them; one tells them to wash their eyes with tea, which takes the dust out and at least costs them nothing and gives a little temporary hope.

We sat and talked to the old man, and heard that it takes a night to walk to Chahcheran along the gorges (about half as long as it had taken us to drive round, but it is possible that *night* here means the twenty-four hours). Mark meanwhile went to examine the river, crowded, he said, with fish. He had not brought his rod for fear of being tempted too much to linger, and we tried to cure this Puritan negation with safety-pins and hairpins for hooks: seven fish had been caught by an earlier party with the lids of sardine-tins cut in strips. But they either rejected our clumsy efforts or swallowed them with impunity, and Mark had the fish to think of, snug and happy inside the noise of their own river, as he lay awake beside them in the night.

The minaret caught the sun above us next morning like a tall opening flower, and we lingered later than usual. On our

way we were to breakfast with the village, for so the Shahrak
Commandant had ordered, and, as they were very uncertain
what sort of breakfast we might like, Zalmia had been asked
to go on ahead and cook it for them.

At the first house by the wayside they took us to sit in a
new room roofed with poplar beams, with panelled walls of
smooth and polished mud; a little hole through the ceiling let
out the smoke – stuffed with a dry bush for the summer –
and *kilims* woven by the women were spread over the floor.
It takes them a fortnight to build such a room, they told us.

They squatted round three walls while we settled on quilts
and cushions along the fourth, and Zalmia and the young men
handed scrambled eggs and our own cups of tea. Conversation
drooped till I asked the only woman present how she managed
to have grey eyes like the English. She was the wife of the host
and of a safe age to sit among men.

"Perhaps your ancestors were cousins of ours?" I suggested.

This fascinating surmise interested everyone and the grey
eyes in Djam were counted. There were vague memories of
people coming from somewhere in the outer world into the
valley; names of Ghurids with no details attached were just
remembered, and the audience was pleased to hear a story
that gave them such a status in their past. "Come again," they
said and waved us on our way.

Except in actual mountaineering where climbing down is
harder, a return is easier in mountain country than an ascent,
and is also less enchanting since one exchanges the hills and
their surprises for the flattening expanses of plains. Even the
difficult corner seemed to have grown easy, and we reached
Shahrak in time to rest and call on the Commandant's wife
and cousin, two women sitting on hard chairs in a lamplit bare
mud room, their beautiful faces medievally framed in white
muslin. All look of frivolity, archness or turbulence disappears

in this nunlike setting, and the presence of a husband and three other men made female conversation practically nil. Claire and I knew we could adjust this in an instant if left to a quiet gossip among ourselves and, finally shifting the men to the other side of the room, plunged happily into clothes, embroidery, and the problem of a baby a year and how to circumvent it (without being too modern), while the men discussed tomorrow's problem of the road.

These charming women had come to their bare village room from the comforts and pleasant companies of Kandahar and were posted, anyway for two years or three and sometimes more, to places as solitary as this or even more so, with none of the active pleasures which the women in our outposts, when we had them, were used to share with their men. That we should *seek* their mountains appears to them very strange, and it is only by talking of important things – children, food, health, religion, and the indestructibly stimulating topic of clothes – that one can build a bridge between our lives.

As for the Herat road, the Commandant had been receiving telephone messages on all hands advising us against it; the Psychologists, he told us, had whirled south in their dust-cloud to avoid the worst stretch by cutting in on to the main road of Kandahar. We, however, were inclined to be obstinate and the Commandant finally said that he himself would choose the Herat road and risk it. Our minds were made up. We were given beautiful presents – stones cut out of the mountains, amethyst and crystal, which the Afghan ladies wear for luck round their necks; and the little family, the four children and the household servants round them, stood with a lantern in their doorway to watch us out into the night.

8

The Second Threshold

The next day of our journey was the crucial one for our Land-Rover. It had to cross the watershed and make its way from the Shahrak Rud, otherwise called the Ishlan valley, to the Hari Rud ford where the gorges are done with and a track from the north and the Murghab country would come down over Parapamisos, with its classic sound, and would run along the level Hari valley by easy going to Herat.

We left earlier than usual, with a last hurried visit to the sick doctor, whose hands were now moist and weak since the fever had left them. To fortify him against contingencies, of which I felt that a great many might be lying in wait for him, I recommended Plotinus who is my chief refuge in trouble, and rather unguardedly quoted George Herbert for the irrelevance of circumstance: "and if the whole world turn to coal" said I, as it seems able to do at any moment, "even then the human spirit in its authentic safety 'chiefly lives'".

"You must say more than that. What does it mean?" he cried, springing round in his bed with much agitation. He was, as I had noticed, philosophically inclined. But the Land-Rover was throbbing downstairs and everyone was waiting; I had to leave him to puzzle out Herbert's view of eternity by himself.

We made west down the river, until doubts began as the path seemed to swerve from our direction, and a lad by some yurts pointed us back to a ford and zig-zags beyond. Cross-currents of rock interlocked across the slope in shallow ridges and when we climbed them and reached the top and looked down, we could see our stream cutting through this range in a short but impenetrable defile evidently impossible to follow. We ground down to its outlet by a number of steep corners, and entered a valley improbable as a dream — white, stained with very faint, sun-bleached, fawn-coloured tints of earth. The anaemic soil must have been made of some malleable substance that shaped itself into small abrupt overhangs, cliffs and hills, held in the greater geographic basin.

We had seen from above a building that looked like one of the old rectangular rabats restored — the only sort of residence likely to remain so completely solitary in the landscape. It had disappeared by the time we reached the valley floor, and there was no other sign of life or labour, except for a small number of human beings squatting listless here and there on their separate gnome-like hillocks, as if they had nothing better to do than to wait for the unlikely passing of a car. They were dressed in the faded colour of their landscape in loose and dingy folds and turbans, and made no sign of greeting, but turned on their heels – on whose support they can squat for hours – to see the last of us along the river track.

I had come to such a pale valley before – one even more naked and deathlike – beyond the swamps of Agheila in Libya, under hills whose crowning cliffs crumbled the white smoothness down their sides; where a signpost stood blank because the rust had eaten it, beside an armoured car of the desert war that had lost itself and died. Nothing was comparably poignant in the Afghan landscape, but there was strangeness only, soon turned to beauty; for we reached the river in the luminous valley, and saw the cliffs reflected in pale distances as our track swerved down into its hollows.

To my mind, rivers and life have always seemed to belong to one another. The wonder of bright water with shadows overarching hit me when I was so small that I had to reach upwards towards my father's hand; since then, I rarely look at a stream without picturing its unseen stretches, the darkness it comes from and the light to which it goes; and rivers and life, Time's pilgrim daughters, seem to me to hold that splendour of transition which is also the inmost happiness and perhaps the beauty of age.

One can share many things with one's loved ones, but not this. To them our removal is a departure, old age a breaking of companionship as the years have made it, a darkness, a humiliation, often an end; in their kindness they try to smoothe it for us, out of sight. But these efforts, to us, are nothing but a discord, involved as we are in so intimate a separation, a disentanglement of which, in the measure of our spirit, the chrysalis within us is aware. It seems right that towards the end of a long journey our interest should be more tender towards the landscape of our life, and towards that intractable, enjoyable part of it that is our own, the imperfect but exquisite machine whose wheels are running down. Yet we need not walk backwards out of Time, in a sterility like that of Lot's wife, fixed on our past; our compelling interest at the turn of the journey must ever be the adventure to come. Through all obstacles we draw near it, and are Ulysses to ourselves. At our prow, the voices whisper from the night; our weaknesses are the tackle of our voyage and Time is our horizon; and beyond it the new horizon must appear: with what eyes we see it, who can tell? At this second threshold, from birth to death, life indeed is such a river as we can watch through the whole of its length at a glance, from source to sea, speedy in its beginning and boundless at its end; and of all natural symbols which the world can write, the flowing stream is nearest to our mood.

In the Afghan journey, through one of the most arid countries imaginable, we were rarely far from the presence of water flowing beside us, and these thoughts came naturally. In my mind's eye I could see the beauty of five rivers already – the peaceful Bamian poured into the stillness of its gorges; and Kabul dropping from ledges towards Indus; and Kunduz eating through the red earth mountains to reach the Oxus and the Aral sea; Panjshir the five-lion river, colour of celadon patterned with foam, muscular as an athlete's corded arm, with the drop of the Hindu Kush behind it; and the wide pasture lands and climbing skylines of Helmand: and we were now hoping to cross into another great valley, that draws tributaries as the tip of the arrow draws its cutting triangle behind it; and we trusted to sleep by the Hari Rud that night.

Meanwhile we lifted ourselves from the white valley, meeting never a wayfarer either with us or towards us, nor any sign of cultivation except a few square patches on far slopes in the sun. We had climbed into a breeze in a cradle of hills held in buttresses and towers of red stone, where neither sheep nor camels could find enough to browse on at this season; the frustrated efforts of the *acantholimon* among its thorns were all the flowers I could see.

From here we dipped and rose and dipped again, and left the red stone and came back to hills churned in cross-currents to a faded dryness where water had run but was now forgotten. Our track petered itself out at a division, and the amateur telegraph poles – rather irregular tree-trunks – which had hitherto acted as a sort of umpire to our doubts, wandered off on a neutral course half-way between the two.

Here, though an actual signpost would probably be used as fuel pretty quickly, one could not help feeling that the *Afghan Tours*, who look after their clients with great care, might have put up a sign of some sort on a stone: ten or twelve Land-Rovers do now make their way through the summer, and without a miracle there is no one within several hours' drive to ask. We deliberated and chose the wrong road, and the two young men began to build it up in its weakest places when the miracle occurred: a greybeard dressed in white, with puttees and sandals of the Himalayan fashion, appeared on a sketchy path round a hill shoulder, driving a loaded black ox and looking as if going from nowhere to nowhere. Like one of those pagan gods disguised, he walked into our story, led us from a night in the wilderness on to our proper path, and faded out very slowly, climbing with his black animal diagonally and alone up a background-slope as smooth and steep as a cataract of rather dirty milk.

The Land-Rover was coaxed westward up a narrow valley. A hut and garden stood uninhabited in a bowl-shaped empty corrie at its head, with its stubble fields around it, and traces

Herat. By the shrine of Gazirgah

Top: Herat to Kandahar. The Russian-built road
Bottom: The tower of Ghazni

Kandahar bazaar

Tower of Mahmud of Ghazni

of rough masonry suggested that a road had been intended. Its zigzags led us up the hills to our watershed, round the western rim of the bowl we had been skirting that tossed in confusion far below. It was one of those traps a hillman will always try to avoid, a rubbish heap of nature, streaked with all colours and devoid of form; and our now liberated road ran happily above it in a breeze that at last could reach us, winding in easy curves along its edge. Its summer-baked surface was already split down the middle, ready to slide with the first rain into chaos, and a small wall placed just where the descending avalanche would detach it seemed a sad little flourish of the impotence of man. One travels on a razor's edge of climate in Afghanistan, between the winter months when the passes are closed, and the spring when the gorges are flooded, and autumn when first rains come: the minaret, we had been told, was accessible only for six months of the year, and none of the tracks we followed were good for a car during anything but summer: our August weather gave our Land-Rover its chance.

Running along the high downlands with villages in sight, we felt that our troubles were over; we looked down slanting lands towards the great east-west valley, sunk out of sight, past Arowā with huts and tents mingled and half its population away on summer pastures; past another charming village with small but welcome clumps of trees; and were told, at a place which seems to be called Margha on the map (the other names were not written at all), that far from having the worst of the road behind us, we had five miles of a torrent fall of boulders to negotiate before we could touch the easy level of the Hari Rud.

We must have reached the descent about two of the afternoon, and the next three hours were spent over these five miles. There had been a road once, but it had been washed away and now overlapped the banks of the torrent that had destroyed it; its entrails hung in tasselled fringes at every one of the numerous crossings, so that it soon became obvious that the only possible thoroughfare was the torrent itself. This meant a very delicate negotiating of boulders on a steep incline, and Mark operated every step with the precautions of a surgeon; Francis called out directions from thirty feet or so ahead, and Zalmia stood ready with his stones, of which there was at any rate a plentiful supply. We had luckily bought a pick in Chahcheran, and could build up a miniature ramp for the most abrupt transitions.

The valley, narrow and not deep, had very little to recommend it; a mere passage for the torrent's caprices, it seemed surprising that even an Afghan engineer with his fatalistic attitude to floods should not have seen that any road here would scarcely stand for a year. The Roman armies used to avoid defiles: how right they were! Lord Elphinstone on the other hand sent out 16,000 men into three of them, one after the other, to their annihilation. But we had nothing but mineral nature to contend with, and that at a time when its forces lay dormant in summer; a little pool here and there and no more remained of the torrent and its rages, and our difficulties lay not with water but with the smooth complex surfaces of boulders, the raw scaffolding of earth battered and stripped and polished by friction, and offering a merely passive resistance, sufficient however to break an axle if Mark once lost his hold. He said nothing – oh wonderful English silence with purpose behind it – but bit his empty pipe-stem and steered slowly, round fold after fold of headlands small and frequent and low, like a congress of crocodile heads between us and the Hari Rud.

As far as I can remember, we had found no suitable place and had eaten breakfast in a tiny plot of shade; and when at last the valley opened, we thought that the ford and our camping place were near and decided to reach it before resting.

The Hari river shone some way off, brightly different from the landscape that contained it, a traveller like ourselves. We had another ridge to cross before we reached it, and the sun was setting when at last the straight bridge and its four pilasters appeared.

Already, where the ford spread smoother water, shadows were curling round its ripples; the western flanks of pebbles gleamed in the horizontal light; and thickets of tamarisk with an avenue of willow trees beyond them lined the flat shore. An easy bank led to a cultivated valley almost free of trees or houses, contained in a distant delicate tracery of rocks.

There was no one about, but we knew what to do, for a chorus of police commandants had begged us not to trust the bridge. One glance along an openwork of holes and tottering girders corroborated this advice, and an old English notice board, equally weatherworn, advised vehicles to unload before crossing. The river itself was about fifty feet wide and not more than knee-deep. Claire and Francis and Zalmia waded over, while the Land-Rover took Mark and me across with slow and crunching noises, and arrows of light and darkness as the agitated current hit our wheels.

9

Nomads

A shouting and clanging, barking of dogs and shifting of
stones under the feet of camels, woke us early next
morning to see the first caravan come down through the
shadow of the hill. The river still flowed softened and dark,
as if under the eyelashes of night, but dawn was about the
upper slopes and a shaft of sunlight hit the long convoy in
midstream as its leader led the first of the reluctant animals
and the water splashed white under their following feet. The

women sat high on their corded bales, uplifted and swathed in draperies like Renaissance madonnas, or those painted in the age of Velasquez for the tall Spanish altars, to look down from built-up thrones that kept them segregated but supreme: not rigidly austere like the Byzantine, but dignified and voluptuous, swaying gently with the swaying hump, in the soft dark folds of their shawls and ample gowns. Some held a child in one arm, while they stretched the other to manage the camel's neck with a long wand of poplar or willow; some had their shifting platform widened with brass or copper cauldrons, mattresses and quilts, beaked coffee pots, or gourds and skins for water, and livestock, new-born lamb, or cats and fowls tied by the leg and settled in any receptacle that had come to hand. The young girls — dark head-veils slanted straight over the full skirt from head to heel — slid from their mounts as they reached the bank we stood on, and helped brothers and cousins to urge and pull and keep the great necks from swinging to right or left; the bigger children already ran alongside with the free bright step of the nomad, their eyes soft and fearless under wild shocks of hair. They kept together in little teams — ready to help as I tried to hand sweetmeats to the smaller ones across the camel backs. The caravan is a living creature, its moods run uniform down all its length, and the women's greetings followed those of the children. "What do you do for security?" an acquaintance had asked in Kabul: "We give sweets to the children," I said, and surprised her, tied up in the bondage of civilization; but the caravan is free of all except its own laws, and moves through the settled lands aloof on its own business, ready like any wild animal to size up its enemies or friends without premeditation.

The beautiful magic swung to the upper valley, and already the second caravan was stepping into the ford; and when that had crossed, the third was on its way. It would take them ten days to reach the lands this side of Herat where autumn would be spent, until winter came and after four months the grass was eaten, and another trek would lead them into pastures near Kalat in Baluchistan.

Everyone has his dream, and who from outside the caravan can tell what its dreams are? To the onlooker, they mean freedom – Ariel calling with all his voices beyond the fear that hides him, the fences that we build.

The nomads too have their fences, higher and more rigid than ours, but they live inside them together with all the world they know, and have no difficult choice to make, while the severity of nature herself presses them into conformity. Their arts must be portable, the same bright patterns with meanings repeated through the centuries, to be stitched on the neckbands of their camels, or woven in rugs and saddlebags and carpets for their tents; or bought in silver amulets and bangles for the wife while she is young, or to wear or sew on to the baby jacket of a son. These are easy things to carry, and no one is much harrowed by a choice. And who has ever seen an 'inferiority complex', or heard of a 'guilt complex' in a nomad? From these symptoms of captivity, traditions that have got mixed and entangled and lost their scale of values, the nomads are immune.

Physical necessities surround them, so that their life coerces them with most of its early vigour, and makes us think them more circumscribed than ourselves; and we sometimes forget that we too are enclosed in walls raised from the darkness of our age, perceptible in the details that make us stumble in our journey – anxieties accumulated from sources unknown or unremembered, divergences of accent or behaviour that show the fences and partitions of our world. Our walls are still those of a cell, however comfortably padded, if we are unable to step out of them and feel at home.

The nomad's wall is too fragile to be a separation, and no doubt he feels this in his obscure heart, since he pines in cities and in captivity is most apt to die. As he walks his sunburnt way or squats in the gathering autumn by some poor fire, he does not feel himself particularly either sheltered or exposed, but is at home in the world like an animal or a plant or a stone – a part of its good and bad caprices.

This ancient harmony sometimes beguiles a city dweller if he knows how to choose his holiday with care. He suddenly feels himself like an instrument in tune; rapture possesses him – no product of knowledge, aesthetic sensibility or learning, but a communion with the roots of earth. It is as if he were given the freedom of the world where his asphalt roads had been rolling him as a stranger. This happens to me sometimes, and I can remember particularly one occasion when I drove from Athens to see friends on the road to Sunium, that circles round Hymettus to the east. There was nothing spectacular, but the brown evening was dripping into the mountain hollow, and I suddenly felt, as I watched it turning under its own sky into the shady night with all its animals – lizards, mice, foxes – asleep in their small caves, that I too was a living part of it, of a home without walls or boundary where anyone might wander, safely because time and life and death had become fused – parts of a single pattern with no great division between them. For a short moment, before I repressed the desire of all my being to leave the road and its traffic and wander into that twilight, I tasted the freedom that the houses have destroyed.

We made a leisurely start when the last of the caravans had departed, and passed and repassed them at intervals through the morning as they crept steadily like caterpillars down the broad flat valley along a route more northerly than ours.

We kept near the river, dipping to its shallow tributaries as we came upon them, where as many camels were browsing

as I had ever seen together, even among the great tribes of
Iraq when they move in the spring. The valley lay dusty in
late summer weather, shorn of its harvests but wide in the
sweep of its water, and shady here and there with groves of
trees and villages asleep. The black woollen tents lined its
banks, for we had left the *yurts* of Central Asia in the mountains and were drifting with the Hari Rud and all its streams
towards the salty marshes of Seistan and the Persian-Arab
world.

The landscape too was sinking on either side of us, rolling
a wide and gentle avenue towards its dusty termination, and
offering no more than manageable cliffs, where a track either
above or below them could be chosen. Black openings of
early tombs speckled their sides here and there. And when
we had crossed two tributaries almost bare of vegetation,
we came upon the headland of Chist and the opening of a
cool oasis that filled a gorge with gurgling water and shade of
mulberries, apples, apricots and willows, so thick-leaved that
the paths there moved in a twilight of their own. On the ledge
above the river, the Ghurids left two tombs and the ruins
of a school decorated with all the solidity and depth of their
thirteenth-century carving, as we had seen it on the minaret of
Djam. Humble, roughly heaped and nameless Islamic graves
lay around, and a modern mosque for pilgrims was not far,
kept in repair and gaudily painted, and founded, they told
us, 'by Sultan Maudad, 920 years ago'. A family of Arabian
ancestry and venerable appearance keeps its tradition alive,
and it evidently draws devotees from a wide stretch of country,
for even Zalmia had heard of it and was able to offer his
devotions while we lingered.

After Chist we again descended. The afternoon was upon
us and we drove through green oases with deserty patches.
The valley sides were too far away to be visible, and drifted

The Walls of Ghazni

The Walls of Ghazni

Ghazni to Kabul

Ghazni to Kabul

with the great watershed westward in a comfortless whiteness of dust in which wind and sun hit us together without mixing, as if contrasting arrows of heat and coolness were tied into one sheaf. Our caravans had vanished, and so had the grazing camels and the tents.

Their virtues and ours too, I reflected, my mind wandering back to the nomads and their values, are very rarely such as a god could share. For there is no *divinity* even in courage, or in six out of the seven categorical – prudence, temperance, fortitude, justice, faith and hope. Courage is not to be practised by that which is irresistible, or prudence by the fountain of wisdom, or temperance by the essence of abundance, nor is there any scope for hope in ultimate beatitude, or for fortitude where no misfortune can ever leave a scar. Who can read *Paradise Lost* without feeling that what we admire most is on the other side? Faith and hope belong to this world only, and patience or justice must be extremely different in their immortal shape. Chastity and obedience are so limitedly human that without love they cease to be virtues at all.

Love and Delight alone may be called immortal and shed their brightness from an unlimited horizon. Through them we share a divine freedom, the temporal enjoyment of temporary things. Any genuine artist or even craftsman can know this in the unpossessive realms where his dreams lead him; any lover must learn to know it as he grows to where self is forgotten. In these two ways of dedication and creation the simplest creature by its own native impulse touches the unchanging shores.

Nomad loves, trudging there in the heat of the valley, are probably no greater and no less than ours; but delight, the other cardinal virtue, is brighter with them because they accept their scanty blessings as gifts and not as dividends, and welcome the mystery from which they come. Respect for the

Unknown we are in danger of forgetting while we plant our flags on the moon; but the nomad is in no danger of forgetting: all that he lives by fluctuates with the kindness or cruelty of the seasons, the births of his camels, the far-away snow that regulates his streams. With needs and possessions so few he cannot bother very much about them, his disengaged attitude to actual objects makes his charm. Even raids and small wars in the long desert summers are a proof and constant reminder of the general fluidity of ownership, and are less indulged in from necessity, I have often thought, than from an unconscious desire to mitigate boredom, which is possibly the basic origin of war. Women, it may be observed, if they managed the world as well as ruling it, would perhaps be better at avoiding wars, merely because they have hitherto been brought up to be less easily bored than men.

The afternoon was slanting towards evening when we reached Obei – wide stubble fields and disconsolate heaps of earth in a cemetery of wind-swept stones before a little settled town that had already a city whiff about it, and what had almost grown to be a whitewashed arcaded bazaar. Here we discovered that some warm springs existed in a cleft of hills now visible in the north. Six miles, said the bazaar, and offered a guide.

We were at the end of a long day and six miles might be anything; but we had been told about the Obei springs, and the thought of a bath was decisive, for the Hari Rud had been too public a river for bathing. We took the guide and were out again in the dust, past a few bending saplings the Obei optimists had planted as a roundabout (in absence not only of traffic but of roads), and across the white emptiness to the hills. In their shelter the wind dropped. A high ridge like lace, silvery as Olympus, showed above us; a steep road, hard and slim, wound along a canyon towards it.

The canyon was loud with the rustling of poplars and splash of the torrent, and lush and green with blackberry bushes that made a tunnel for the stream. The road, like a fairy tale, led on and on beside it, until it opened a small amphitheatre where five rooms decorated with blue and white and yellow stood in a row against the rise of the mountain, and let its springs gush into five pools of cement through hand-hammered pipes of brass or bronze. The warm dark water coiled and splashed perpetually, on to a slightly sunken platform where one paddled on blue tiles, and the stream found an escape through the drainage of the floor. On the hillside close above, under a zig-zag of pines, was a small hotel. There were no other visitors, but the baths were attended by a conscript soldier who spent his days cleaning and rinsing and taking, as far as I can remember, twopence from every bather. Our clothes we washed and hung out on the amphitheatre's attempted rose garden, and climbed in the dusk to our *pilau* at the hotel. Here four or five carpeted rooms, not furnished but ready in their civilized way for visitors who come travelling with the necessities of life in their baggage, breathed a refinement, now dimmed and forgotten, of the high and sophisticated world from which it came. But who first built the baths – some prince of Herat one would imagine – we were not able to discover: the sound of their water tumbling through the five pools floated through our camp under the pine trees in the dark.

10

The Western Roads to Kabul

This was our last night with the Land-Rover in the open. The suburbs of Herat were only four hours away and the flattish but bumpy Obei track that led to them soon widened to an earth road where we saw our first urban car that was neither jeep nor Land-Rover nor lorry. We were down now at little over three thousand feet and villages spread their harvests. Early names are mentioned by Ptolemy and others, and the fertile habitations go back into an unrecorded past. Sights to which we had become accustomed in small individual mountain nests, here by mere size took on the majesty of age: the *juy* grown almost to a canal ran out of sight for miles beside its line of willows; the cultivated stretches almost touched each other towards the riverlands; where the sowing stopped the hard earth had become a threshing-floor and great communal drums of corn were pulled down by the villagers in diminishing diameter as the black oxen trod the people's harvests from generation to generation for ever. The only modern object in sight would be a metal jerry, which some child ran to hold beneath an animal when it needed it, to prevent the wetting of the corn.

The last of Parapamisos, a low and dusty range, was also now descending on our right into the salty deserts below Merv. In a large village called Paliberi the *bad-girs* appeared – square towers above the roofs, with slits to let north winds blow down into the houses. We were in the Persian atmosphere, as different as possible from the unsoftened Afghanistan of the east. As we neared the suburbs, we reached hillsides and avenues of pines where the army and a number of pleasant modern homes were scattered and hidden in shade; and from a low rise the whole oasis spread before us, dark green against a deserty horizon, with its four faint-pencilled minarets clustered together in the sun.

Herat is one of those places that illustrate geography: it must exist as long as the river spreads itself to feed it. Old-Persian Hairova, re-named Alexandria-in-Asia, its feminine suffix (*at*) supplied by the Arabs, it lies like Balkh in a lowland where the trade routes were bound to pass – a situation made for constant destruction and resurrection. Coming from Djam, what interested us most was its growth under the Ghurids, who built the great mosque (A.D. 1201) a year before their minaret. The tomb of its founder is now being renovated in one of its many annexes, and a splendid door, turquoise glaze and brick, buried under the later Timurid architecture, has just been discovered.

The Mongols blasted Herat in 1221 and again in 1222, but the people returned, and a Kurt, or Kart, dynasty (Tajik and related to the Ghurids) ran their administration for them till Tamerlane destroyed it. Under his descendants, and especially under Husain Beg Baiqara in the early sixteenth century, Herat reached its climax of wealth and splendour and became the richest and most civilized city in Asia. Babur visited his cousins there after he had conquered Kabul, and devotes many pages to its famous and learned men, to picnics in summer houses – of which the baths of Obei are probably a poor descendant – and to the gay young princes who could teach him how to carve a goose and tried to make him drink wine, but had no knack with armies.

The Uzbeks were marching down from the north, and Babur, as we have seen, crossed the Kuh-i-Baba to defend his capital. Herat was again captured, and nearly two centuries followed of Uzbek and Persian and finally Afghan-Persian rule. When in 1747 Afghanistan came to be governed by its own people, the struggle continued in a wider field, between the greater powers – Palmerston and Nesselrode, England and Russia, polite but wary in the background; Persia and north-west India on the stage. In 1837 Lord Palmerston's protest broke the Persian siege of Herat; in 1856, when it had again been pounced upon and captured, the British rescued it with a three-months' war; and in 1863 it was taken over and joined to the main body of Afghanistan by Dost Muhammad, whose vicissitudes during our first two Afghan campaigns had finally ended in friendship.

Geography is behind trade, and trade is behind history, and this sequence should ever be remembered: a dispatch from St Petersburg in 1838, when these affairs were simmering, refers to the 'indefatigable activity displayed by English travellers to spread disquiet among the people of Central Asia, and to carry agitation even into the heart of the countries bordering on our frontier whilst on our part we ask nothing but to be admitted to partake in fair competition the commercial advantages of Asia.'*

Nothing can save Herat and Kandahar from being the only western approach to Kabul and India south of the Hindu Kush even with modern transport, and we thought of this geographic fact when we sped along the Russian-built highroad to meet the American-built highroad at Kandahar. Meanwhile we enjoyed Herat in its historic lull, as so many have done before us.

Claire and Mark had already driven here from Persia, and took us to a hotel only moderately modern and shaded in a garden. A leafy twilight drenched it, and carpeted corridors dimly vaulted were scattered with large bathrooms infinitely soothing. Francis had rushed off and been lucky enough to see dervishes dancing in the mosque; his time was up and he had to leave, and his hired jeep had broken down tactfully before starting; Zalmia rescued him with a bus ticket and we saw him off into the sun, with a night and day's ride before him. We then relaxed, and drove through miles of shady avenues, through the one-storeyed street that looked Persian enough under trees, to Gauhar Shad's minaret and tomb. That great woman of the Herat renaissance left a dome at Meshad and many good works behind her before she was murdered. Her buildings and those of Baiqara, clustered at this end of

---

* Clanricarde to Palmerston 20.11.1838: quoted by Fraser-Tytler p.104

the town, were levelled by the advice of some British military advisor in 1886 to make 'a field of fire' against a Russian attack that never came. Only the minarets remain, four crooked fingers not unlike factory chimneys in the bareness of their surroundings, yet melting, pale turquoise and white mosaic, into the heaven they belong to. Not many years can pass before the last of this beautiful ornament must drop away.

We went again next morning to photograph and examine the pattern, for the white borders give it a silvery fragility that needs the sun as if it were a flower. Even so, the 'field of fire' was not open enough for Claire's picture: seeing a suitable roof, we knocked and explained ourselves to a kindly family of women, whose gardener and ladder helped us to a view. Other women, strolling in the Gauhar Shad shades, welcomed us too; they gathered with heads covered but faces unveiled to ask how we liked their city and invite us to their houses. The doves cooed in the trees, in the pleasant oriental atmosphere of a civilization that has forgotten to be rich. One would like to stay longer in Herat.

The citadel, with only one fine mud-tower left intact, has less of such feeling than Gazirgah, a quiet cemetery beyond the suburb gardens, where Baiqara lies under a tomb so intricately carved and slenderly intermingled, one would think the wind could lift its tendrils of black stone: yet the artist's grip never falters or loses its purpose, weaving it as a writer his words, who tries to keep them steady on their way. The stone is closer than words to the short hard brilliance of Khurasan.

There for a moment, as time goes, the civilization of Persia was strengthened by the Turkish stream; the Ghaznevids, the Ghurids, the Timurids lived with taste and splendour on the road of the Indian trade, of which they held the keys from Punjab to the Oxus at both ends. Mahmud of Ghazni, echoing the forgotten Greeks, brought up his 1700 elephants through the southern passes; collected slaves and sold them, 2–10 dirhems apiece; and sat in his hall on his red-gold throne, overlaid with Byzantine brocade.

When the Mongols had come and gone, after their spoliations, Ibn Batuta in the fourteenth century found Kandahar intact and Herat recovered. And Tamerlane rose and passed. And their hour came for his descendants also, when they had beautified the sophisticated city and learned the Persian ways: and carved the black stone with the harvest of the ages behind them, so that it remains intact and still belongs to the constructive world.

> They will trample our gardens to mire, they will bury our city
>   in fire;
> Our women await their desire, our children the clang of the
>   chain,
> Our grave-eyed judges and lords they will bind by the neck
>   with cords,
> And harry with whips and swords till they perish of shame or
>   pain,
> And the great lapis lazuli dome where the gods of our race had
>   a home
> Will break like a wave from the foam, and shred into fiery rain.
> No more on the long summer days shall we walk in the
>   meadow-sweet ways
> With the teachers of music and phrase and the masters of dance
>   and design.
> No more when the trumpeter calls shall we feast in the
>   white-light halls,
> For stayed are the soft footfalls of the moon-browed bearers of
>   wine.
> And lost are the statues of Kings and of Gods with great
>   glorious wings,
> And an empire of beautiful things, and the lips of the love who
>   was mine.

We have vanished, but not into night, though our manhood we
    sold to delight
Neglecting the chances of fight, unfit for the spear and the bow.
We are dead, but our living was great; we are dumb, but a
    song of our State
Will roam in the desert and wait, with its burden of long, long
    ago,
Till a scholar from sea-bright lands unearth from the years and
    the sands
Some image with beautiful hands, and know what we want him
    to know.[*]

*   *   *

We left early on August 18 for our two last and hottest days.
The Russian road covers the 555km. where the winds of
Seistan from their blistered spaces can reach it at a hundred
miles-per-hour.

We had slept by our Land-Rover in a corner of the hotel
garden, and at five in the morning the kettle was already
making its pleasant noise. Mark was choosing sheltered places
for our cushions, fixing the car for its journey, slipping away
when all was done to come back shaved and neat. Claire and
I, so well looked after, had our diaries to catch up with. A
cool dry wind ran with the dawn and a silvery crescent moon
was waning over the pines.

When we were well out of Herat the sun rose yellow as
butter, and everything grew small before it. Low reptile ranges
pushed through the sand, and broad pale valleys flattened
themselves between them. Patrick Balfour[†] drove here in
a Rolls-Royce in the thirties, breaking the bridges over a
weary three-day stretch which the straight Russian arrow now
pierces, punctuated by two petrol stations and a hotel. The

[*] *Pillage:* J. E. Flecker
[†] Now Lord Kinross. *Grand Tour:* (John Long)

villages are almost invisible, so poor and far between, and as the day advanced we watched the flatness increase until hardly anything but the scarcely perceptible curve of earth was left us, over a surface of small gravel and hard sand.

We lunched in a patch of shade on a small terrace where a friendly platoon of soldiers were stationed. The road was like a course ploughed by ships in an empty sea, and in the late afternoon threw us up a little derelict from among its plunging lorries – Italians in a baby Fiat whose axle (or something equally vital) had given out on the concrete, where they had been sitting for two days asking drivers to take them back to Herat for nothing: they had English friends in a Morris who came up to us for help. No one would think it anything but silly to climb the Matterhorn with a frayed rope or useless shoes; but these young adventurers who have not lifted a finger in study or preparation think it nothing to live off people poorer than themselves when they reach that inexorable moment when two and two make four. A lorry, we explained, would definitely have to be paid for, probably overcharging; but we would do our best to find one for Herat at the next stopping-place.

Meanwhile the evening light began to gather; the sun no longer filled up all the sky. It hung like a yellow ball above its goal, and the desert pebbles glittered in its rays. The evening coolness was falling, and in the villages women were fetching water (not one had been visible in the hot hours): outside the tea-house, the lorry drivers sat on the ground at ease, their dust-coloured clothes spread about them. There was nothing to be done to make them move in any direction but their own: the little Fiat would have to follow necessity to Kandahar.

Inland, on the skyline, a jagged lacework of hills was appearing. Caravans of firewood, and cows in long lines returning, moved beside us along a far-stretched avenue of pines; they were making for the city in the dusk. Kandahar itself appeared,

abruptly cradled in rocks, with cliffs and patches of green water; and the avenue turned in to where the quick-trotting
tongas were out with all their tassels. A young boy, his motor
cycle leaned against a tree, was putting his forehead to the
asphalt for the evening prayer; a park with Christmas-tree
lamps in its trees appeared and our hotel beside it.

The best skull-caps and waistcoats and fine white shirts are
still stitched and sold in the bazaars of Kandahar. We spent a
short hour among them next morning and set out on our long
day, east of the Helmand valley and down again to Kabul along
the American asphalt of the fourth road in Afghanistan. On the
almost imperceptible watershed sits Ghazni with two carved
minarets a little less graceful and a little earlier than the minaret
of Djam. Her great gate, then supposed to be impregnable,
was stormed by Colonel Dennie of the 13th Light Infantry in
1838, and is now closed to tourists because of barracks behind
it. But I had seen it the year before, wandering all over the
markets beneath its splendid wall.

"I am afraid you cannot photograph, because it is a military
object," a handsome young officer had said to me in English
as correct as his uniform.

"Can I photograph *you*, if I can't take the gate?" said I.

"No," said he, laughing: "I too am a military object."

We parted with, I think, perfect understanding, and I had
to wait for my photograph till he had turned the corner.

This time almost the whole area was forbidden, and we
were not sorry to press on over the 334 miles that had been
the record of Lord Roberts and his army in a march of three
weeks and two days. Late in the afternoon and far in the north,
fair and unattainable, we could see Kuh-i-Baba, its pastures,
flocks, and small cradled cornlands with their villages and
towers, almost invisible in the hurrying lorries' dust.

Index